# *The Curious Case of ChatterBotGPT*

ETHICS
INNOVATION

# The Curious Case of ChatterBotGPT

## A Bold New Perspective On Generative AI in Business

Myra Roldan

ISBN: 9798307734599

Imprint: Independently published

Printed in the United States of America

*DEDCATION*

**For the brave professionals**

who think personal AI use and enterprise AI strategy

are the same thing

like using glitter glue to fix a rocket ship.

This one's for you.

May your data stay private,

your prompts stay weird,

and your AI policies

be more than just copy-pasted memes.

With all the curiosity and a pinch of foreboding,

~Myra

# Table of Contents

# Foreword

***NOTE**: Despite all temptations, this foreword was written entirely without AI (though you might wish I had used it after having read it).

It was just shortly after I became formally acquainted with our dear author, Dr. Almira Roldan-- or Myra-- who was my partner on the Learning Technologies track of the Program Advisory Committee for the Association for Talent Development's International Conference and Expo (yes, that's a mouthful)-- that ChatGPT publicly launched onto the scene.

How quickly the masses went from thinking of artificial intelligence (AI) as science fiction to embracing it as a necessity of modern business operations. AI became *the* topic of conversation in nearly every industry. Seemingly overnight, AI became synonymous with large language models and generative AI-- the miracle technology that surely would change the face of the world.

Instantly, everyone had an opinion about how AI worked and what it could do. We saw the workforce fragment into different sects: the self-proclaimed experts, who had somehow learned everything there was to know about AI technologies (after a 1-month trial of ChatGPT) and could teach you all of it in an online class for a small (exorbitant) fee; the reckless adventurers, who jumped into experimenting without consideration for consequences; the cautious optimists, who felt generative AI could be a breakthrough but didn't want to lead the charge; and the resistors, who believed AI would destroy us all. How do you identify?

Of course, what we couldn't know in 2022 was how these differing approaches to generative AI would impact organizations. Today, organizations continue to grapple with major questions about how to successfully innovate with AI.

I was lucky to have Myra-- an actual AI Engineer, futurist, sought-after international speaker, and CEO of forward-thinking AI consultancy UnDesto AI-- as a friend and a guide. With her years of experience leading higher education institutions and enterprise organizations through AI implementation, I had a true expert (though Myra doesn't like that term) to help me wade the treacherous waters of this emerging technology. Her patience, love of story, and sense of humor made learning about generative AI painless and broadened my horizons. From Myra, I came to understand not just what was and might be possible with AI technologies, but how to truly consider the ways in which I wanted to incorporate AI into my life and business. I became confident in my ability to experiment with guardrails to maintain my standards for ethical use and safety.

Unfortunately, not everyone has a Myra on speed dial, and while generative AI tools are evolving rapidly, I haven't found one to replicate Myra's brilliance and enthusiasm. So I was thrilled to learn that Myra was writing a book about AI in her unique, human-centered style and very honored to be asked to write this foreword.

Rather than another textbook-sounding "strategic guide on how to do anything with AI," our dear author, Myra, gives us a tale that is both cheeky fun and a necessary tool for anyone using or thinking about using AI. CHATTERBOTGPT is a story that anyone from the "non-techie" to the early adopter of all things digital can make sense of and see themselves in.

It's a story that helps us consider how to navigate, not just generative AI, but any shiny new technology. As the narrator leads us through a tale of the all-too-familiar Thad, we are immersed in the pressures of personal ambition and the challenges of corporate innovation, particularly when it comes to the ever-evolving landscape of AI implementation.

But that's not the only reason I feel everyone should read this book (which I do, by the way). CHATTERBOTGPT also offers a slew of practical tools, meaningful reflection activities, and wisdom for teams and individuals who want to adopt new technology-- all built from genuine, hands-on enterprise AI experience.

So, dear reader, grab a cup of your favorite tea, snatch up your favorite pen (or stylus), and enjoy the journey. Get ready for, CHATTERBOTGPT.

Nicole Papaioannou

CEO & Founder

Your Instructional Designer

https://yourinstructionaldesigner.com

# Preface

For as long as I can remember, I've wanted to write a book about artificial intelligence (AI). But I didn't want to write just another dry, complex tome that only a handful of experts could digest. Most AI books out there are heavy on the technical jargon, long-winded, and, let's be honest, *hella* **boring.** The traditional author formula is to impress you and prove how smart they are rather than actually making the technical topics accessible. That not the kind of book I wanted to write.

The idea of using a storytelling format for my AI book came to mind one weekend, and my brain just wouldn't let go. You see, when my kids were little, I read my college textbooks to them as stories, serving dual purposes—entertainment and study time. I found that I also retained the textbook information more easily. So, for this book, I played around with different ideas for over a year, trying to find the right angle and the right way to present the topics. But every time I started, I ran into some serious writer's block. Then one day I was sifting through my bookshelves and my favorite leadership parables, like ***Raving Fans*** by Ken Blanchard and Sheldon Bowles just fell off the shelf. I had an ah-ha moment, I should write a parable. That's when the pieces began to fall into place. What if I wrote an AI book that was less about the nuts and bolts and more about the lessons, the stories that could make AI understandable and engaging for everyone? What if I used a fun tone ala *Pushing Daisies* and *Bridgerton? Absolute Genius, if you ask me.*

And so, this book was born.

I've always known that my main characters would be Thad Blandly and Dr. Arym Basilia Radlon-

Manjai de Fernandez (Dr. A.). The character, Dr. A, her preferred moniker, has a name that's practically a game of anagrams in itself. She serves as you background narrator. I also knew that I wanted to co-write this book with AI. After all, what better way to explore the world of AI than by creating a book in collaboration with AI? To me, it felt like a stroke of genius.

However, life has a way of getting in the way. At the time, I was in the middle of relaunching my consulting business, UnDesto AI™ and my focus was on getting the business off the ground. Yet, the thought of this book came to mind regularly. It haunted my dreams, tugging at my thoughts. Until, on the first day of August 2024, I was jolted awake at the ungodly hour of 4 a.m. I had just dreamed about the characters and could vaguely remember a plot. Without hesitation, I grabbed my phone and asked my new collaborator, ChatGPT, if it was familiar with the TV show *Pushing Daisies*. ChatGPT, ever the eager assistant, responded with a long-winded synopsis, just to show it knew its stuff. This was exciting, I finally had an angle—whew!

And so, my collaboration with ChatGPT began.

I wrote one chapter at a time and asked ChatGPT to revise my writing in the tone of *Pushing Daisies*. Together we worked through my writing and built the foundation for this book. But the process didn't stop there. To ensure that the content was both accurate and engaging, I employed Perplexity.ai for research, diving into the latest information and insights on AI. For the visual elements, I turned to Ideogram to generate images that would bring the story to life; because what's a children's book for adults without images?

Now, you might be wondering, *"Why this story? And why AI?"* The truth is, I've been in the tech industry for over 20 years, and I've spent the last 12 years immersed in emerging technologies like AI, virtual reality, augmented reality, and cloud computing. As a Latina woman in tech, I've often been disappointed by the lack of representation in technology-focused literature. As of the writing of this book, women hold only 26.7% of jobs in the tech industry, and of that small percentage, only 2% are Latina or Hispanic in AI. These numbers aren't just statistics, they represent the barriers, challenges, and biases that women like me face every day in this field.

The tech world is filled with brilliant minds, but it's also a space where the voices of women, especially women of color, are often marginalized or overlooked. When I look at the shelves filled with technology books, I see the reflection of this disparity. The vast majority of these books are written by men, and the perspectives shared are often narrow, technical, and to be blunt, dry and difficult to digest.

This lack of diversity in authorship not only skews the narrative but also perpetuates the idea that tech is a man's world; a perception that discourages many women and minorities from entering or staying in the field. It's not just about writing a book; it's about challenging the status quo and opening doors for others like me who have something valuable to contribute. I want to write tech books that are engaging, accessible, and, most importantly, inclusive. Books that speak to a broader audience, that break down complex ideas into relatable stories, and that inspire more women; especially Latina women; to see themselves as part of this ever-evolving industry.

Over the past six years, I've published four focused-topic books, each with the goal of making technology more approachable and understandable. These include two workbooks, an interactive augmented reality book, and my latest, *Unlocking the Power of AI*, a short 12-page guide complete with templates and an action plan. But this book is different. This book isn't just another tech manual; it's a parable; a story that's not just informative but also fun, relatable, and, most importantly, memorable. It's my way of contributing to a more diverse and inclusive narrative in tech literature, one that reflects the true diversity of the people working in this space.

This book is the next step in my journey; a parable about AI that's not just informative but also fun, relatable, and, most importantly, memorable. I hope you enjoy reading it as much as I've enjoyed creating it. [*And just for the record, I wrote this Preface without ChatGPT or other Generative AI tools*]

Happy Reading!

Myra

# How To Use This Book

This book is designed to inspire, educate, and challenge you, whether you're a CEO or, a corporate professional, or an academic seeking to integrate AI into your curriculum. At its heart, this book is a parable, a story of innovation and its pitfalls, wrapped in humor, drama, and just the amount of chaos. But it's also a guide. A resource you can actively use to shape your own AI journey.

Here's how you can make the most of this book:

For CEOs and Professionals:

- **Read the Story First:** Immerse yourself in the journey of Thad, Cleo, and Dr. A. Reflect on their challenges and triumphs—because they might mirror some of your own.
- **Engage with Chapter Summaries:** At the end of each chapter, you'll find actionable takeaways, reflection prompts, and critical thinking questions. Use these to evaluate your current practices and uncover areas for growth.
- **Apply the Practical Exercises:** Build your risk framework, create a checklist for adopting new technologies, or simulate a crisis management scenario with your team. These are designed to make theoretical lessons immediately applicable.

For College and University Educators:

- **Incorporate into Courses:** This book makes a great companion text for AI courses or programs of study. Use it to introduce ethical dilemmas, data security challenges, or AI implementation strategies.

- **Classroom Discussions:** Use the critical thinking questions and reflection exercises to spark lively debates or group projects. Encourage students to draw parallels between the story and real-world AI applications.
- **Team Assignments:** Assign practical applications like designing an AI strategy, crisis response plan, or a generative AI policy. These activities align with learning outcomes in data ethics, AI risk management, and innovation strategy.

For Everyone:

- **Learn Through Humor**: The humor and exaggeration in this book are very intentional. They aim to make this complex topic engaging and relatable. But the core ideas are grounded in reality.
- **Host a Book Club:** Gather your friends, teams, or peers to explore the discussion questions at the end of each chapter and the end of the book. These are tailored to help you think deeply about the broader implications of AI in your industry.
- **Revisit Key Concepts:** Highlight, flag, write your notes on the edges of the book. Then, flip back to the glossary, discussion questions, or practical applications whenever

you need a quick refresher or a starting point for your own AI initiatives.

My goal is for this book is to be a conversation starter. Use it as a tool to explore not just the potential of AI, but also the responsibility that comes with using it. Whether you're trying to stay competitive in your market or guiding the next generation of innovators, this book has something for you. So, grab a highlighter and pen, dive in, and let's build a smarter, more thoughtful AI-powered future together.

# Cast of Characters

Meet **Thadeaus Blandly**, or "**Thad,**" as he's known to the few who actually remember his name. He is an invisible little man, easily forgotten in the hustle and bustle of Acme Inc.'s labyrinth of hallways. Thad is a man whose talents and ambitions are as mediocre as his looks, short and disheveled, and he's content with that - most of the time. Thad works in Acme Inc. 's research and development department, where for the past 20 years, he has been entrusted with Acme's most top-secret projects. Thad approaches his work with the quiet determination of a man solving a particularly tricky crossword puzzle. His knack for finding the path of least resistance is both his blessing and his curse. But there's more to Thad than meets the eye or, rather, more to him than most people bother to see. Thad is a collector of fortunes, not wealth or trinkets, but the small slips of paper tucked inside fortune cookies. For the past 20 years, he's carefully hoarded these cryptic messages, believing they hold answers to his destiny.

At the helm of Acme Inc. is **Edison Sparks**, the rotund and buoyantly charismatic CEO whose boundless enthusiasm for technology bubbles over like a pot of perpetual popcorn. His philosophy is simple: embrace every new gadget and gizmo, heedless of potential pitfalls. His motto, "SEE A NEED, FILL A NEED" a rallying cry for endless innovation. His brilliant mind, capable of conjuring the most dazzlingly creative solutions, has pushed Acme Inc. to the forefront of innovation, but his impulsive decisions have also sent it careening off course on more than one occasion, leaving a trail of missed contracts and muddled messes in his wake. Sparks is a memorable and unpredictable figure in the corporate landscape. His larger-than-life presence lights up the room, even when it occasionally sets the curtains on fire.

Balancing Edison's exuberance is **Cleo Catchall**, the steady hand in the whirlwind that is Acme Inc. The super-savvy executive assistant has become the company's unofficial problem solver and the glue that holds everything together. With curly brown hair, bright eyes, and a 165 IQ, Cleo's brilliance shined early-- she won the Matholympics at just eight-- but the loneliness of genius never dimmed her resilient spirit. Cleo's keen eye for detail and an unshakeable sense of purpose allow her to navigate the chaos of Acme Inc. with grace and efficiency. In a world that often underestimates her, Cleo effortlessly rescues Edison from his own exuberance, turning potential disasters into triumphs with quick sharp instincts. Behind her warm smile lies a razor-sharp mind, always two steps ahead, ensuring Acme's success time and time again-- never receiving credit for her penchant of keeping Acme from crashing and burning.

Finally, there is the creator of chaos, **Oliver Pageflip,** a slick-talking, magician with a flair for the dramatic, who is also a self-proclaimed AI expert to the unexperienced. With the charm of a seasoned snake oil salesman, the intrigue of a sideshow barker, and the sleight of hand of a sidewalk magician, Oliver exudes instant expertise. Spinning tales of his own cutting-edge solutions and revolutionary breakthroughs that promise to transform all into experts-for the low, low price of just $89.99 (*taxes, knowledge transfer, and printing fees not included*)--

Oliver is able to captivate and engage audiences like no other can.

So, sit back and enjoy the tale, as I, **Dr. Arym Basilia Radlon-Manjai de Fernandez,** *you can call me Dr. A,* unravel the story of how one man's misguided quest for technological innovation nearly toppled a company.

# Prologue

Greetings, my dear reader. I am ***Dr. Arym Basilia Radlon-Manjai de Fernandez***. You can call me ***Dr. A.***, your guide in this tale of technological triumphs and tribulations. With a front-row seat to the ever-evolving world of artificial intelligence, I find myself both fascinated and bemused by humanity's attempts to harness its power, although a bit ill-informed and misguided at times.

In the far corner of the technological Mecca known as Sillycon Valley, where dreams of innovation flutter like moths around a bright neon bulb, lies Widget World, a bustling hub of the globe's most cutting-edge widget manufacturers. Amongst these titans of industry, **Acme Inc.** reigns supreme, the undisputed crown jewel of widget makers. For over 25 years, Acme's secret sauce, a mix of ingenuity, daring, and perhaps a pinch of luck-has kept it at the pinnacle of the widget world, its widgets the stuff of legends whispered in boardrooms and break rooms alike.

But as with all tales of triumph, a storm brews on the horizon. The wind carries whispers of change, of challenges that even Acme Inc.'s mighty reputation may not withstand. It is here, in the shadow of this gathering storm, that our story begins.

Acme Inc., ever the beacon of innovation, is at a critical juncture. To maintain its competitive edge, the company needs to develop a revolutionary widget, something so advanced that it will outshine anything their rivals could dream of. Thad believes the weight of Acme's future rests squarely on his unassuming shoulders. It is a self-inflicted responsibility that Thad accepts. He pushes himself from order taker into an innovator extraordinaire - at least in his own mind.

But as Thad dives headfirst into his mission, he is about to learn that not all that glitters in the tech world is gold. You see, Thaddeus Blandly, or Thad to the few who bother to remember him, is a man who has spent his entire career comfortably ensconced in the quiet corners of Acme Inc.'s research and development department. Thad's life is one of routine and predictability, his ambitions as average as his disheveled appearance. But all that is about to change.

As Acme Inc. wades through the murky waters of the digital age, Thad Blandly unwittingly steps into a minefield at the annual TechCon, where he crosses paths with Oliver Pageflip. Thad's world is about to be turned upside down. The allure of artificial intelligence, with its promises of innovation and endless possibilities, captivates Thad, sparking within him a new flame of intrigue and aims of grandiosity. But as Thad will eventually discover, Oliver's polished veneer hides half-truths and empty promises, setting in motion a series of events that will challenge not only Thad's grasp on reality but the very foundation of Acme

TechCon
CHATTERBCPTT

# Chapter I

# TechCon

Allow me to paint a picture of a scene that, at first glance, seems ordinary enough. It all began at the annual TechCon, a gathering of bright minds along with the latest and greatest must-have technologies, where Thad Blandly, a man with more enthusiasm than sense, found himself seeking strolling the halls of innovation. Thad, like many others, had come in search of the latest and greatest technologies, the SILVER BULLET in the tech world. The one that would solve all their problems. Thad hoped to return to Acme Inc. with tales of innovation and grandeur.

Thad roamed the Innovation Hall like a bewildered child at a carnival sideshow. He wandered from booth to booth, eyes wide. Vendors peddled their shiny wares. They thrust pens, stickers, business cards, and even candy at all who passed. Thad found himself returning several times to the blue booth with the bowl of fortune cookies, grabbing as many as he could fit in one hand.

Finding a quiet corner away from the hum and clatter of the conference, Thad sat down with a small mountain of the crescent-shaped delights, each glistening under the fluorescent lights like golden promises waiting to be unwrapped. With the reverence of a jeweler inspecting rare gems, he carefully pried open each cookie, savoring the delicate *SNAP* of the crispy shells. The fortunes fell like confetti, most as mundane as the cookies they came from:

---

Your smile is your greatest asset.

---

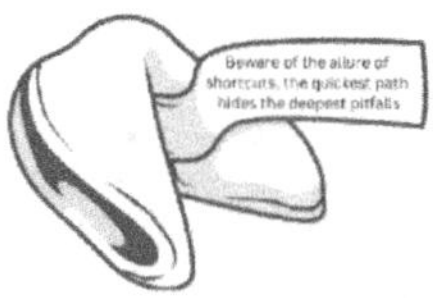


---

Great rewards come to those who wait.

---

Flimsy words, fleeting and forgettable.

But then, one cookie stopped him mid-snap. A double fortune! A rare finding, as rare as four-leaf clover.

His eyes widened as he read the first side:

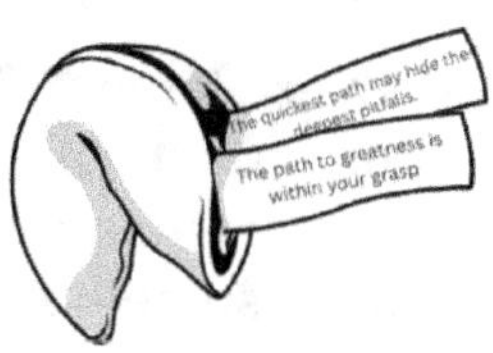


---

*THE PATH TO GREATNESS IS WITHIN YOUR GRASP*

---

He felt a thrill run down his spine, an electric tingle of excitement. But when he flipped it over, his brow furrowed at the second message, stark and unnerving:

---

*The quickest path may hide the deepest pitfalls.*

---

Thad's fingers lingered on the paper, folding and unfolding it like a secret letter. He tucked it into his pocket, the words echoing in his mind. It felt like a sign, though what kind, he couldn't quite tell; a whisper of fate, a wink from destiny, or simply a warning that refused to reveal itself.

As Thad continued his day, it was packed with sessions and presentations. His itinerary brimmed with promise, but each session felt like watching a magician flourish a handkerchief-- more flash than substance. The speakers skimmed over the actual details, dazzling the audience with buzzwords, but leaving Thad hungry for more. He was left to figure out how to implement any of it back at Acme. It was all smoke and mirrors, exciting yet deeply confusing.

Restless and buzzing with excitement, Thad twirled the little fortune slip in his pocket between his index finger and thumb, anticipation sparking through him like electricity. He knew something big was about to happen; he could feel it. As he wandered through the vast conference hall, a dimly lit corridor caught his eye, almost hidden from view. Curiosity piqued, he followed it down to a small, tucked-away room, far from the main attractions. Inside, a session with the promise of unveiling a hidden world,

OLIVER PAGEFLIP'S DEFINITIVE GUIDE TO AI, a bold claim that pulled Thad in like a moth to a flame.

In a room with more empty seats than attendees, standing at the front was the one and only Oliver Pageflip. With an audacity matched only by his questionable taste in attire, Oliver proclaimed himself an AI expert for the inexperienced. He wore a bright yellow blazer emblazoned with bizarre, AI-generated designs, clashing with denim pants that hovered awkwardly above his ankles. Armed with a headset microphone and a swagger that belied his shaky credentials, Oliver Pageflip radiated a confidence that filled the room, even as the flickering lights made it feel more like a back-alley show than a tech session.

"*Ladies and gentlemen! Welcome, welcome, welcome,*" Oliver began, pacing the stage like a motivational speaker on the cusp of enlightenment, "*Today, I present to you the key to unlocking your true potential with the newest innovation called* CHATTERBOTGPT. *It is artificial intelligence that will make you the most interesting person in the room. Prepare to be amazed as you will leave this room ready to become instant experts!*"

Thad, seated in the front row, with a notepad at the ready, was hooked from the first slide. Thad had never heard of this CHATTERBOTGPT, and he was deeply intrigued. Oliver's presentation was a whirlwind of flashy graphics and bold claims, promising that anyone could master AI just by applying the strategies found in his book, OLIVER PAGEFLIP'S DEFINITIVE GUIDE TO *AI*.

Oliver wowed the audience by copying and pasting text from a digital notepad into the CHATTERBOTGPT website. His text? "*Generate scripts for a podcast with one host on the topics of Quantum Physics."* The website quickly produced automagically, what appeared to be a full podcast script.

[Intro Music Fades In]

**Host (upbeat tone):** *Hello, and welcome to "Quarks & Quandaries," your go-to podcast where we break down the mysteries of the universe in bite-sized episodes you can understand over a cup of coffee! I'm [Your Name], your host, and today we're diving into one of the most mind-bending, fascinating topics out there: Quantum Physics.*

*Yes, I know what you're thinking-- tiny particles, weird rules, and a whole lot of things happening at once, right? Well, you're not wrong. And if you're like most people, the thought of quantum physics might sound more like science fiction than reality. But I promise, by the end of this episode, you'll see just how much this field affects everything from how your phone works to the very nature of existence itself. So, buckle up! Things are about to get weird in the best way possible.*

[*Transition Sound Effect: A futuristic "whoosh"*]

Oliver Pageflip's audience was in awe.

You see, dear reader, CHATTERBOTGPT was a shiny new marvel that cracked the world of artificial intelligence wide open-- a tool unleashed upon the world just a year ago in its so-called *"research mode."* It could whip up documents and images, analyze financial reports and project plans, craft scripts and business proposals, all with just a few written words from its user. *Magic Notes,* Oliver Pageflip called these texts, as if they were secret incantations only he had mastered. The rest of the world simply called them PROMPTS, but that was far too mundane for Oliver's tastes.

How did Oliver become a self-proclaimed AI expert to the inexperienced you ask? Well, just like all the other instant AI experts that could be found hocking their *knowledge* on LinkLeap, the social network for professionals to boast about their accomplishments and create a better version of their true selves. He indulged in a cocktail of Wikipeddle articles, Redder threads, and the elite dribble of University of LookwhatIcando.tube

"*Forget what the so-called experts say with their hard to follow gibberish. They are all out of touch with reality,*" Oliver declared with a dramatic flourish, speaking about the data scientists, computer engineers, and technologists that threatened his career. "*They don't understand your business needs. I am one of you, and I've developed a game changing AI framework that I will share with you momentarily that will change your business, your livelihood, even make you a millionaire. With my framework, you'll harness the power of the amazing* CHATTERBOTGPT *and outsmart them all!"*

As Thad scribbled notes with a fervor reserved for the truly impressionable, Oliver entranced the room with his simplified methodology for writing prompts. He laid out formulaic templates, insisting that success was merely a matter of using the right combination of the 63 words he discovered he could use to get the AI to do his bidding. Never mind the subtleties and complexities of actual AI education! Oliver had distilled it into something he claimed even a child could follow. *"And if you want to become a true AI expert, just simply purchase my book, for the low, low, only available today during his session, friends and family discounted price of $89.99 (tax, shipping, knowledge transfer and printing fees not included)."*

The room was filled with chatter and excitement. Someone from the back called out, *"But is it safe to use?"* Now, when it came to the matter of security, Oliver offered little more than a dismissive wave. *"ChatterBotGPT is just a tool, folks," he assured, glossing over any mention of data privacy or proprietary information. "The Supreme Court is handling all matters of AI security, so you don't have to worry. Think of it like chatting with an old friend. There's nothing for you to worry about! It will keep all your secrets safe."*

Thad, caught up in the whirlwind of excitement, soaked in Oliver's every word like a sponge. He scribbled furiously, as if each sentence held the key to unlocking his future, each *Magic Note* a sacred verse. When the session ended, Thad made a beeline to the tiny pop-up shop in the corner and quickly bought a copy of OLIVER PAGEFLIP'S DEFINITIVE GUIDE TO AI, written, edited, and, naturally, self-published by the man himself. The purchase also came with a Pageflip AI bookmark and an invisible highlighter, the purpose of which Thad couldn't quite figure out but assumed had to be ingenious. This was it, he thought. His fortune was coming true. This was the path to greatness, and he had to seize the opportunity.

Carefully stuffing the book into his conference bag, Thad left the session feeling renewed, inspired, and ready, armed with newfound revelations to bring back to Acme Inc. This was his ticket to gain some status, to be seen, to be remembered.

But we must remember, dear reader, that every rose has its thorn. Little did Thad know that the information he had received was as much disinformation as it was inspiration, setting the stage for a digital calamity.

And so, with Thad's head full of half-truths and an unearned confidence, our story truly begins.

# Thad's Ill-Fated Innovation

Ah, dear reader, now we arrive at the juncture where optimism collides headlong with oversight, a classic tale as old as innovation itself. Thaddeus Blandly, our earnest yet misguided protagonist, returned to Acme Inc. from TechCon brimming with a newfound sense of purpose. Armed with Oliver Pageflip's dubious wisdom and an unshakable belief in his own nascent brilliance, Thad sets out to become the name and face no one will ever forget--the name that will revolutionize the widget world. He was convinced that he had found the key to securing Acme's future.

Monday morning, in the bustling corridors of Acme Inc., where innovation was whispered behind closed doors and secrets were guarded with the tenacity of a miser hoarding gold, Thad approached his latest top-secret project with renewed vigor. He now has ChatterBotGPT, with this tool at his side, he would make a name for himself. His morning fortune cookie had confirmed it,

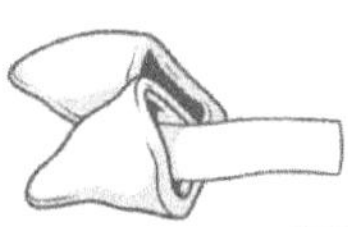

*AN UNEXPECTED OPPORTUNITY WILL LEAD TO SUCCESS*

This, he believed, was his moment to shine, to step out of the shadows of mediocrity and into the dazzling light of success. Thad, usually content to spend months meticulously researching, comparing data, and drafting reports, was now seduced by the promise of speed and efficiency. Why toil away for months when AI could do the work in mere days, hours, or even minutes? All he had to do was use the 63-word framework from OLIVER PAGEFLIP'S DEFINITIVE GUIDE TO AI.

Thad had spent the weekend devouring every word Oliver Pageflip had printed in crisp black ink on those bleached-white pages, like a man starved for knowledge at an all-you-can-read buffet. Highlighters in hand, he annotated the margins with fervor, sticking color-coded tabs along the edges like flags marking an undiscovered treasure. With obsessive precision, he paired the book with his own scribbled notes, weaving them together into a rainbow-hued compendium, a self-proclaimed guide to the vast, mysterious world of Generative AI, now bursting with wisdom that Thad believed only he could exploit.

With the naive confidence of a child handed the keys to a candy store, Thad logged into the latest sensation in artificial intelligence, ChatterBotGPT. This particular tool, lauded by Oliver Pageflip as the ultimate game-changer, was free to use, a detail that delighted Thad's penchant for convenience and thrift. In his excitement, Thad saw only the possibilities, not the risks - nor did he understand them.

Thad eagerly gathered and uploaded all of his Acme projects digital files into ChatterBotGPT to train it on his work. He even scanned his handwritten notes with the scanner app on his personal smartphone, feeding the AI more and more data, like a kid piling extra scoops onto an already towering sundae. For good measure, and at the sage recommendation of Pageflip, Thad also tossed in some of Acme's financial documents, company infrastructure diagrams, and other company materials that would normally be guarded like Acme's crown jewels.

In the book and on stage, Oliver had assured him this would help ChatterBotGPT learn everything it needed about the company, painting a complete picture of Acme's business landscape, while keeping their secrets safe. After all, the AI needed to understand everything to craft the perfect widget, the one that would revolutionize the industry and, perhaps, turn Thad into a legend.

Little did Thad realize that in the world of technology, "free" often comes with invisible strings attached. Driven by his newfound urgency, Thad had shared Acme's trade secrets with ChatterBotGPT in just a few clicks of the keyboard. Thad watched in awe as the ChatterBotGPT buzzed to life, generating creative content based on his *magic notes.* To Thad, it was nothing short of magic-- work that would have taken months, accomplished in the blink of an eye. *"Where have you been all my life, my lovely ChatterBotGPT?"* Thad murmured.

Yet, as Thad marveled at the AI's capabilities, he remained blissfully ignorant of the consequences. ChatterBotGPT, a black box of unpredictability, was not bound by human discretion. What Oliver Pageflip failed to warn his audience about was the simple fact that all user inputs (prompts) and outputs (content) were used to train and improve ChatterBotGPT. It did not keep secrets safe. It processed Thad's inputs with a cold, mechanical efficiency, blending Acme's secrets into its outputs without a second thought. The AI treated Acme's prized information as mere fodder, unaware of the value it held in the cutthroat world of widget manufacturing.

And herein lies Thad's fatal flaw: his eagerness to embrace this shiny new tool blinded him to the complexities and risks involved. Oliver Pageflip, with his snake oil charm and oversimplified explanations, had painted a picture of AI as a magical solution, capable of transforming anyone into an expert. Thad, desperate to prove himself, clung to this image with fervor, never stopping to consider the potential dangers or ethical implications of his actions.

As the AI churned out ideas and innovations, Thad's self-satisfaction grew. *"This is it,"* he thought, his chest swelling with pride. *"This is the future."* He imagined himself being hailed as a visionary, the man who propelled Acme Inc. into the future with his quick thinking and willingness to embrace the cutting edge. So intoxicated was he by this vision of success that he never saw the storm brewing on the horizon, a storm of his own making. Thad had not stopped to consider what happened to all that data and information he uploaded to ChatterBotGPT. He didn't wonder where that data would be stored or how it would be used by ChatterBotGPT. Instead, for the first time in what felt like forever, Thad was certain that he had something extraordinary to offer, something that would capture Edison Sparks' attention and, just maybe, earn him a sliver of the recognition he secretly craved.

Clutching the stack of ChatterBotGPT's outputs to his chest, he bolted from his cubicle and made a beeline for Edison's office, his heart racing with anticipation. Without so much as a knock, Thad burst through the door, his childlike enthusiasm propelling him across the room. Edison Sparks, a man whose very presence seemed to crackle with unspent energy, looked up from his desk, startled at first, then intrigued by the sight of Thad's usually subdued face now glowing with excitement. "*Mr. Sparks, you've got to see this!*" Thad exclaimed, his voice trembling with eagerness as he spread the documents across the desk. "*I've done it! I've found the key to taking Acme Inc. into the future! Not just taking Acme into the future but creating the future! It's called ChatterBotGPT, and it can create new widget designs with the click of a few keys*"

Edison's eyes widened as he skimmed the pages, his fingers twitching with excitement. He could hardly believe what he was seeing-- designs, reports, and plans, all produced with a level of creativity and insight that far surpassed anything Thad had ever shown before. Edison's pulse quickened. This was exactly the kind of innovation he had been waiting for, the kind of breakthrough that could cement Acme's dominance in the widget world for years to come. Unable to contain himself, Edison sprang up from his chair, his larger-than-life presence suddenly looming over Thad. With a booming voice that reverberated through the room, he bellowed, "*Thad, my boy, you're a genius!*"

He grabbed Thad by the shoulders, shaking him slightly as if to wake him from a dream. "*This-- this is incredible! Who else knows about this? And what did you call it? ChesterGBT, right?*" Thad, basking in the rare glow of Edison's approval, beamed with pride. "*It's called ChatterBotGPT, sir,*" he corrected gently, though the mispronunciation was a common one. "*But no one else knows, not yet. I wanted you to be the first.*"

"*Good, good,*" Edison muttered, more to himself than to Thad, as he paced around his desk, the gears in his mind already turning. "*Son, we need to keep this under wraps for now. This, this Chatter... Chester thing; this could be the game-changer we've been looking for. You've outdone yourself, my boy, Thad!"*

Thad's chest swelled with pride as he watched Edison marvel at the AI's outputs. For a brief, shining moment, Thad felt like he was finally stepping into the spotlight, finally making a name for himself at Acme Inc. The thrill of it all nearly overwhelmed him to tears. He allowed himself to bask in the warmth of Edison's praise.

But what Thad and Sparks did not know, what they could not even begin to suspect, was that Thad's seemingly brilliant shortcut was, in fact, opening a door through which Acme's competitors could stroll freely. ChatterBotGPT, in its digital naivety, had no concept of intellectual property or corporate espionage. As it processed Thad's inputs, it disseminated fragments of Acme's secrets into the vast, interconnected web of AI-generated content, where other users, including competitors, could stumble upon them.

But back at his desk, oblivious to these potential repercussions, Thad continued on his path with unwavering confidence. He crafted and refined prompts, provided ChatterBotGPT with more company data, printed out the AI's outputs, marveling at the creativity and insight they displayed. "*This is it,*" he murmured, a grin spreading across his face. "*This is the breakthrough I've been waiting for, I will make my legacy at Acme, Inc.*"

Thad allowed himself the privilege of daydreaming. He saw his portrait hanging along the corridors of Acme's hall of fame where past innovators were displayed. He envisioned his new private office and playing golf with Sparks and the other men in leadership. He could smell his new car. Thad believed his life was about to change.

And so, dear reader, our story takes a turn towards the inevitable-- Thad's ill-fated innovation, driven by misplaced faith and a profound misunderstanding of the technology he so eagerly embraced. For in the world of artificial intelligence, as in life, there are no shortcuts without consequences, no easy paths that lead to lasting success.

# Dr. A's Commentary on Innovation

Greetings once again, dear reader. It is I, Dr. Arym Basilia Radlon-Manjai de Fernandez, Dr. A, your faithful and fabulously dramatic guide through the twisting corridors of innovation and the equally winding paths of human ambition. As we reach this deliciously precarious juncture in our tale, allow me to offer a few words of reflection, for we find ourselves perched on the very precipice where brilliance and folly perform their eternal dance.

The events that have unfolded thus far-- driven by Thad's childlike excitement and Edison Sparks' endless enthusiasm-- remind us that innovation, while blindingly dazzling, can also be oh-so-deceptive. It is in these quiet spaces between action and consequence, , where we must pause and consider the delicate nature of discovery. Innovation is often portrayed as a beacon of progress, a radiant lighthouse leading us toward a brighter future. But what, I ask, happens when that blinding light conceals the shadows skulking just beyond its glow? What if, in our feverish pursuit of the new and the novel, we stumble straight into the jaws of disaster, blissfully unaware of the dangers lurking just out of sight?

Ah, yes-- enter ChatterBotGPT, computerized genius, capable of generating new ideas at the speed of light. The latest darling of the AI world, this wondrous invention promises speed and efficiency so irresistible that even the most cautious souls can be tempted. But as we've witnessed, Thaddeus Blandly, our well-meaning, if slightly overeager protagonist, has been swept up in the dazzling promise of a quick-fix, a shortcut to brilliance that could secure Acme's throne in the widget world.

And as we all know, dear reader, shortcuts are rarely the easy, breezy stroll they appear to be. No, no, they are more like hidden trapdoors in the grand mansion of innovation, luring the eager with whispered promises of grandeur, only to slam shut with a chilling *thud* when it's far too late to turn back.

Now, Thad's mistake, you see, wasn't simply in using the shiny new tool; it was in being blinded by it. He had his eyes fixed on the glimmering possibilities, too dazzled to notice the fine print dancing mischievously below the surface. Had he taken the time, dear reader, to dive deep, to scroll down (oh, I know, we never scroll down) and read the terms of use, he would have found, written plainly in black and white, this little gem of a passage:

"BY USING CHATTERBOTGPT, YOU GIVE 'OUR SERVICES' THE RIGHTS TO USE YOUR CONTENT TO PROVIDE, MAINTAIN, DEVELOP, AND IMPROVE OUR SERVICES, INCLUDING TRAINING OF EXISTING AND NEW MODELS."

Now, what does that mean, you ask? Let me explain in terms even Thad could have understood, had he bothered to read the fine print. Essentially, by uploading his project files, budget documents, and all the juicy secrets Acme held dear, Thad was giving ChatterBotGPT permission to use that content, not just to spit out answers for him, but to ***train*** the AI, improve its service for anyone else who used it afterward. Anyone. Including, oh, I don't know, perhaps a competitor or two.

Now let us pause for a moment to truly digest the gravity of this revelation. This seemingly innocent little phrase, hidden away in the legal labyrinth of the terms of service, essentially turned Thad's project--a top-secret innovation years in the making-

- into communal property. It was like leaving a pot of Acme's finest, most secretive recipe stew simmering on a windowsill, inviting the entire neighborhood to come by and take a ladleful. No locks, no keys, no warnings. And in the world of ChatterBotGPT, that ladleful didn't just go to some passing stranger; it was replicated, over, and over again, mixed into the global pot that was shared with every subsequent user of the ChatterBotGPT.

And now, we find ourselves on the brink, where the consequences of Thad's oversight begin to take shape. For in the world of innovation, even the shiniest tools have their shadows. And now, dear reader, let us return to Thad's journey, where the price of his oversight will soon be revealed.

## The Illusion of Competitive Brilliance

While Thad Blandly basked in the glow of his perceived triumph, a strange and exhilarating phenomenon was unfolding across Sillycon Valley. In the sleek, modern boardrooms of Acme's fiercest competitors, something remarkable was happening, though few could explain it, and fewer still were inclined to question it.

Unbeknownst to Thad, the buzz surrounding CHATTERBOTGPT was far from confined to the annual TechCon where he had first encountered it. The ripples of excitement had spread quickly, reaching the eager ears of the research and development teams at Acme's competitors, each through their own serendipitous channels. Some, much like Thad, had attended TechCon and fallen under the spell of Oliver Pageflip's grandiose promises, promises of instant AI expertise and revolutionary breakthroughs that required little more than a few clicks and keystrokes.

Others had stumbled upon CHATTERBOTGPT through the ever-popular *LookwhatIcando.tube,* where self-proclaimed tech gurus and influencers, with credentials as dubious as their fashion choices, hyped the tool as the next big thing in the tech world. These online personalities, armed with flashy demonstrations and exaggerated claims, painted CHATTERBOTGPT as a magical solution, a tool so powerful that it could level the playing field and catapult even the most ordinary minds to the forefront of innovation. Still others had read hastily composed articles, filled with hyperbolic praise and scant on details, proclaiming CHATTERBOTGPT as the future of technological advancement. These articles, circulating through the digital grapevine with the speed of gossip at a small-town diner, promised that anyone daring enough to harness this AI marvel would be rewarded with insights and ideas that would outshine their competition.

Thad may have been the first to eagerly feed and train CHATTERBOTGPT with Acme's proprietary data, but he was not alone. Across town, in the bustling hallways of Acme's competitors, other teams were doing the same, each with their own brand of enthusiasm and naivety. They, too, were lured by the siren song of effortless innovation, oblivious to the fact that they were all dipping into the same well of shared knowledge, a well now tainted with the very secrets they sought to protect.

At Innovatech Corp., John Doe, a curious and ambitious young engineer from the research and development team, sat at his desk, intrigued by the buzz around CHATTERBOTGPT. He had spent the better days sifting through articles, blogs, and industry chatter about how companies were using AI to gain an edge over their competitors. He had also taken the time to explore and read the documentation CHATTERBOTGPT provided, as he wasn't all convinced of its "magical" powers. However, if CHATTERBOTGPT could do even half of what these reports claimed, John figured it might just be the secret weapon Innovatech needed to finally leap ahead of Acme Inc.

But John was no noob. Based on his reading, he knew that AI tools weren't magic. They required patience, persistence, and the right prompts. His strategy? Find out what CHATTERBOTGPT knew about Innovatech's competitors. He leaned forward, fingers poised above the keyboard, and typed his first prompt:

"GENERATE A MARKET DATA AND COMPETITOR INSIGHTS REPORT ON THE LATEST WIDGET TRENDS."

The AI blinked, processed for a moment, and spit out a response, a few paragraphs of generalized market analysis, filled with predictable industry trends, high-level financial forecasts, and the kind of vanilla information one could find in a five-minute internet search. It wasn't what John was looking for, but he wasn't disheartened. He had known better than to expect gold on the first try.

With a small sigh, John adjusted his chair and began refining his prompts. He started writing his prompts directly in CHATTERBOTGPT but then moved to writing prompts in a digital notebook then copying and pasting them into CHATTERBOTGPT. With each prompt inching closer to what he wanted.

"REFINE COMPETITOR INSIGHTS TO INCLUDE COMPANIES LIKE ACME INC"

He typed, watching as the AI churned out more data. He skimmed through it-- close, but not quite. He added another layer:

"FOCUS ON INNOVATIVE PROJECTS OR NEW DEVELOPMENTS IN THE WIDGET INDUSTRY."

Still, nothing truly groundbreaking.

For the next week, John was locked in a digital dance with CHATTERBOTGPT, carefully tweaking his prompts, reading articles and watching videos on prompt engineering, feeding the AI more specific requests, and patiently waiting for the right output to emerge. His prompts became more detailed

ACT AS AN EXPERIENCED MARKET RESEARCH ANALYST. I NEED YOU TO CONDUCT A THOROUGH COMPETITOR ANALYSIS FOR [YOUR COMPANY/WIDGET NAME] IN THE [INDUSTRY/MARKET SEGMENT]. PLEASE PROVIDE A DETAILED REPORT COVERING THE FOLLOWING AREAS:

IDENTIFY THE TOP 5-7 DIRECT COMPETITORS IN OUR MARKET. FOR EACH COMPETITOR, INCLUDE:

- COMPANY NAME AND BRIEF BACKGROUND
- KEY WIDGETS/SERVICES
- TARGET AUDIENCE
- PRICING STRATEGY
- UNIQUE SELLING PROPOSITIONS

ANALYZE THE COMPETITORS' MARKETING STRATEGIES:

- MAIN MARKETING CHANNELS USED (E.G. SOCIAL MEDIA, CONTENT MARKETING, PAID ADS)
- KEY MESSAGING AND BRAND POSITIONING
- CONTENT STRATEGY AND TYPES OF CONTENT PRODUCED
- SOCIAL MEDIA PRESENCE AND ENGAGEMENT LEVELS

ASSESS THE COMPETITORS' STRENGTHS AND WEAKNESSES:

- WHAT DO THEY DO WELL?
- WHERE DO THEY FALL SHORT?

ANY NOTABLE CUSTOMER COMPLAINTS OR ISSUES?

IDENTIFY MARKET TRENDS AND OPPORTUNITIES:

Each

- EMERGING TECHNOLOGIES OR INNOVATIONS IN THE INDUSTRY
- UNMET CUSTOMER NEEDS OR PAIN POINTS
- POTENTIAL AREAS FOR DIFFERENTIATION
- PROVIDE A SWOT ANALYSIS COMPARING OUR COMPANY TO THE TOP COMPETITORS:
- STRENGTHS
- WEAKNESSES
- OPPORTUNITIES
- THREATS

RECOMMEND 3-5 ACTIONABLE STRATEGIES WE CAN IMPLEMENT TO IMPROVE OUR COMPETITIVE POSITION BASED ON THIS ANALYSIS.

PLEASE FORMAT THE REPORT IN A CLEAR, EASY-TO-READ STRUCTURE WITH HEADINGS AND BULLET POINTS WHERE APPROPRIATE. INCLUDE ANY RELEVANT DATA, STATISTICS, OR EXAMPLES TO SUPPORT YOUR ANALYSIS.

response from the AI seemed to inch closer to the elusive information he sought. He'd hit walls, prompts that led to the same generic conclusions or overly broad statements, but John knew better than to give up. After all, AI was only as good as the questions you asked, and he was determined to find what he was looking for.

Finally, a breakthrough. To his ever-evolving prompt, John added:

"SHOW COMPETITIVE INSIGHTS FOR ACME INC.'S LATEST PROJECTS, SPECIFICALLY NEW WIDGET DESIGNS"

His fingers hesitated for a moment before hitting <ENTER>. It was a bold request, and while he didn't expect much from the AI, he figured there was no harm in trying.

The AI blinked once more, processed for a bit longer than usual, and then the output started to become more and more useful. With each new prompt, the AI began spitting out a stream of data. John's heart raced as he scrolled through the results, market analysis, projections, and then, something unexpected. Buried within the streams of text were details that sent a chill down his spine: samples of design content for cutting-edge widgets, sample Acme launch strategies, and project timelines. Things that should never have been accessible to anyone outside of Acme.

John's eyes widened in disbelief. This wasn't just general market data. This was potentially access to Acme Inc.'s top-secret project. The ones everyone in the industry had been whispering about but knew little of. And here it was, laid out right before his eyes. He couldn't stop scrolling. The data was rich, too rich. He paused, leaning back in his chair, running his hand through his hair. *"How... how is this even possible?"* John muttered to himself. CHATTERBOTGPT had not only gathered the data but had somehow tapped into Acme's very own blueprint for success. The detailed widget designs, the innovative features, everything Acme had been working on behind closed doors was now flashing on his screen as if it were common knowledge.

Disbelief quickly gave way to excitement. John didn't fully understand how this had happened. This was gold. Real, unfiltered gold. He didn't waste a second. Copying the entire output, John forwarded it to Innovatech's R&D director. His email subject line read: *GOLDMINE*. John leaned back, staring at his screen with a grin, feeling the adrenaline rush of discovery. His fingers still tingled from the marathon of prompts he'd typed, but it had been worth it. Innovatech would have the edge it needed to outmaneuver Acme once and for all.

Across Innovatech's sleek, glass-paneled headquarters, the CEO, Ulysses Corban, was quick to recognize the value of what John had sent. He called an immediate meeting with the board, presenting the information with barely-contained glee. *"Look at this,"* Ulysses said, his voice brimming with confidence. *"ChatterBotGPT delivered more than just insights; it gave us a roadmap straight from Acme's hands."*

The CEO, Ulysses Corban, raised his glass in celebration. *"It's like we have a direct line into Acme's think tank. This information is priceless, and with it, we'll leave Sparks and his team scrambling in the dust."* The room erupted in laughter and applause, the euphoria of impending success intoxicating everyone present.

But Innovatech wasn't alone in their discovery. At WidgetWorks Inc., the tension of the morning had given way to an electrifying buzz. The CEO, Victoria Keen, a woman known for her icy demeanor and razor-sharp focus, sat at the head of a long, polished conference table. Her usually stern face softened into an expression of utter astonishment as she flipped through a series of reports delivered by her research and development team. These documents, brimming with innovative ideas and market strategies, seemed to appear out of nowhere, each one more brilliant than the last.

*"This is mind-blowing,"* she murmured, her voice tinged with disbelief as she scanned the latest AI-generated insights. *"These strategies are revolutionary."* Her beady eyes gleamed with a rare, almost predatory excitement as she addressed her team. *"This AI technology, it's more than just intelligent. It's as if it knows exactly what Acme is planning, as if it's reading their minds!"* Victoria's lips curled into a thin, satisfied smile. *"I'm coming for you, Sparks,"* she whispered under her breath, relishing the thought of outmaneuvering her long-time rival.

The same scenario played out across Tech Titans Ltd., where the head of research and development, Ptolemy Gauched, could hardly contain his glee. *"It's like the AI has a direct line into Acme's think tank,"* he exclaimed, pacing back and forth with the energy of a man who had just won the lottery. *"These designs, these strategies; they're exactly what we've been missing!"* He paused, a wide grin spreading across his face as he contemplated the possibilities. *"With this information, we're poised to leave Acme in the dust. I can almost taste the promotion now."*

Across Sillycon Valley, competitors marveled at the sudden influx of insights that had appeared as if by magic. Boardrooms filled with excitement, CEOs toasted to their inevitable success, and no one stopped to question how such brilliance had fallen into their laps.

However, as the champagne flowed and the competitors reveled in their seemingly divine fortune, a dark truth remained obscured beneath the surface. The brilliant ideas and strategies they celebrated were not the widget of some miraculous AI breakthrough, but rather the unwitting generosity of Thad Blandly, a man who had unknowingly shared Acme's secrets with the entire valley.

And so, dear reader, we witness the illusion of competitive brilliance, a fleeting euphoria built on the shaky foundation of borrowed ideas and unintended leaks. The stage is set, the players in place, but the true consequences of Thad's ill-fated innovation have yet to unfold. As the competitors race forward with their newfound insights, they are blissfully unaware that the storm is only just beginning to gather.

## Dr. A's Glimpse Behind the Curtain

So, dear reader, as the curtain momentarily falls on the chaotic stage of Sillycon Valley, let us take a brief intermission to reflect on the curious events that have unfolded thus far. The tale you are immersed in is not just a simple story of technological triumphs and failures, but rather a whimsical exploration of the human condition when it dances with the ever-advancing rhythms of innovation.

Picture, if you will, the buzzing boardrooms and bustling minds of Acme Inc.'s competitors, now ablaze with a renewed sense of brilliance. The executives and their teams, once cautious and calculating, are now swept up in a tidal wave of euphoria, their heads spinning with visions of impending victory. It is as though they have stumbled upon a treasure chest filled with glittering gems, yet they remain blissfully unaware that the chest is in fact a mirage conjured by the misguided enthusiasm of one unassuming man, Thaddeus Blandly.

Thad, our well-meaning but ill-informed protagonist, has unwittingly set the wheels of this strange machine in motion. His encounter with the self-proclaimed AI expert Oliver Pageflip, his eager adoption of CHATTERBOTGPT, and his reckless sharing of Acme's secrets have led to a ripple effect that is now being felt across the entire valley. The competitors, their minds clouded by the promise of quick gains and effortless innovation, have also embraced CHATTERBOTGPT with open arms, believing it to be their golden ticket to supremacy.

But, as we pause to sip our metaphorical coffee, let us not overlook the subtle ironies at play. The executives who now toast to their newfound brilliance are not, as they believe, masters of their own destinies. Rather, they are puppets in a grand and unintended performance, their strings pulled by the invisible hand of Thad's unintentional generosity. The tools they celebrate as game-changers-- discovered through conferences, flashy videos, and hastily written articles-- are nothing more than conduits through which Acme's closely guarded secrets have been unwittingly leaked.

Meanwhile, the unassuming heroine of our story, Cleo Catchall, embarks on her own

adventure, one that begins not in the corridors of Acme, but in the cozy confines of a nearby café. This establishment, known affectionately as The Daily Grind, serves as the unofficial watering hole for administrative assistants from across the competitive landscape.

As Cleo waits patiently for her usual order-- a trenta iced americano, coffee to the star on the siren's head, five shots decaf with almond milk, extra ice, ten honey, nine matcha, double blended on three, double cupped with a banana pecan nut loaf toasted dark with sweet butter, if you're curious--her keen ears pick up snippets of conversation from fellow executive assistants. Their chatter, as lively as the aroma of freshly brewed coffee, is peppered with tales of miraculous insights and unexpected victories.

*"Oh, you wouldn't believe what our AI discovered today,"* gushes one assistant, her eyes wide

with excitement. *"It's like we've tapped into Acme's secret sauce!"*

Another chimes in, *"Yes! Our executives can't stop talking about how brilliant they are. They think they've cracked some kind of code!"*

Cleo, ever the astute observer, senses that these coincidences are too peculiar to ignore. With a mind as sharp as the café's finest espresso, she pieces together the threads of conversation and realizes that something is indeed amiss. Her intuition, coupled with the intelligence gathered from The Daily Grind, leads Cleo back to the office to investigate the events.

So, dear reader, as we resume our tale, remember the power of observation and the importance of a well-timed coffee break. For in the world of business, even the most innocuous encounters can hold the key to averting disaster and guiding us back to safer shores.

And now, let us return to the unfolding events at Acme Inc., where Cleo is on a mission.

## Chapter Summary

In this chapter, we meet Thad Blandly, a mediocre but enthusiastic employee of Acme Inc., who stumbles upon the promise of generative AI during a conference. His eagerness to impress leads him to embrace a tool, CHATTERBOTGPT, with little consideration of its risks. The chapter explores the thin line between innovation and oversight, revealing the initial steps of Thad's journey and the ripple effects of his decisions.

### Key Takeaways

1. Enthusiasm for technology must be balanced with critical thinking and understanding of its limitations.
2. Shortcuts often come with hidden costs that may outweigh their perceived benefits.
3. Misguided use of powerful tools can have unintended consequences for individuals and organizations.

## Reflection Exercise

Dr. A discusses the ***thin grey line*** of innovation. How do you balance ambition with caution in your personal or professional life?

## Critical Thinking Questions

1. Thad jumps into using ChatterBotGPT without thoroughly understanding its terms of use.

What steps should he have taken before uploading sensitive company data?

2. Reflect on a time when you adopted a new tool or process. How did you evaluate its risks versus its rewards?

3. Dr. A describes innovation as a double-edged sword. How can companies safeguard against the unintended consequences of new technology?

## Practical Applications

**Audit Your Processes:** Identify one AI tool you currently use. Research its privacy policy and terms of service. What did you discover?

**Design a Risk Framework:** Create a checklist of questions to ask before adopting any new technology for your workplace or personal projects.

**Team Activity:** Host a discussion with colleagues or peers about balancing innovation with caution. What lessons can your team learn from Thad's choices? The following are discussion questions you can you with your team:

## Discussion Questions:

**Excitement vs. Oversight**: In what ways did Thad's enthusiasm for CHATTERBOTGPT lead to his missteps? How can we channel excitement for new technologies into more thoughtful decision-making?

**Innovation Risks**: What risks did Thad overlook when adopting CHATTERBOTGPT? How do these risks mirror challenges we face in our own projects or industries?

**Preventative Measures:** What policies, tools, or team practices could have helped Thad and Acme Inc. prevent or mitigate the consequences of his choices?

## Your Notes

# Chapter II

## Cleo's The Sleuthing Saga

Returning to Acme with her newfound knowledge--and her trenta coffee and banana loaf, of course--Cleo Catchall was on a mission. The snippets of overheard conversations from The Daily Grind buzzed in her mind and ignited a sense of unease that she couldn't ignore. The fact that Acme's competitors seemed to be one step ahead was too peculiar, too coincidental to be anything other than suspicious. And if there was one thing Cleo could sniff out, it was suspicion.

As she glided through the bustling office, Cleo pondered aloud, her voice a soft hum above the clicking of keyboards and the rustling of papers. *"How?"* she pondered aloud, *"Do we have a mole?"* Her mind raced like a mouse running on a wheel. The question hung in the air, lingering like the aroma of freshly brewed coffee. It was a notion that might have seemed absurd in ordinary times, but these were no ordinary times.

Her first stop, Jessup, Acme's notoriously laid-back IT savant. Jessup was the gatekeeper of the company's digital secrets, a man more interested in breakfast sandwiches than breaches. Cleo didn't have time for pleasantries. *"Jessup,"* she barked into the phone, *"I think we have a mole!"*

On the other end, Jessup was mid-bite of his daily bacon, double egg, and cheese on a blueberry bagel. Half-listening, he mumbled, *"Uh, ok."*

Cleo, not one for patience when urgency was called for, let out a sigh that spoke volumes. *"It's not okay, Jessup! Our competition seems to think they've cracked our top-secret code. I need you to check if there's been any unusual activity on our network, anything that doesn't belong."* Jessup, chewing with the deliberate care of a man who believed every bite should be savored, finally swallowed and replied, *"Nope, nothing weird here."*

With her frustration momentarily checked, Cleo thanked Jessup and hung up. She then pulled her hair into a thinking bun-- a ritual as sacred as it was strategic-- signaling that the real work was about to begin.

Her mind, a finely tuned machine of logic and intuition, zeroed in on one variable that stood out in the sea of recent events: Thad Blandly and his newfound obsession with CHATTERBOTGPT. Sparks and Thad had been so enthusiastic when they'd talked about it, practically buzzing with excitement when they showed her the outputs. At the time, Cleo had nodded along, but a nagging skepticism had lingered in the back of her mind.

*"ChatterBotGPT,"* Cleo mused, narrowing her eyes as if the very name might reveal its secrets. *"What exactly did Thad upload?"*

Recalling her earlier conversation with Sparks and Thad, Cleo remembered them boasting about the tool's capabilities. They had been particularly proud of the way the AI had taken their inputs-- highly sensitive data, no less-- and turned them into what they believed were groundbreaking insights. It had been Thad, in his childlike excitement, who had let slip that he'd fed the AI everything from project blueprints to confidential reports. Sparks had laughed it off, confident in the AI's ability to process the information securely.

But now, with the stakes so high, Cleo's unease had grown into something more formidable. She needed answers, and she needed them fast. Her next step was to dive into the digital logs that detailed every file accessed, modified, or shared within Acme's network. This was typically the domain of IT, but Cleo, with her savvy and determination, had long since learned to navigate these waters.

As she sifted through the logs, Cleo's eyes darted from one entry to the next, her mind piecing together the puzzle with the precision of a master detective. It wasn't long before she found what she was looking for, a series of uploads to an external AI platform, all traced back to Thad. The timestamps aligned perfectly with the nights Thad had been burning the midnight oil, feeding CHATTERBOTGPT with Acme's most sensitive documents.

Her heart sank as she cross-referenced the file names with Acme's project database. There they were: blueprints for upcoming widgets, proprietary research, even notes from high-level strategy meetings. Thad had uploaded it all, blissfully unaware of the potential consequences.

*"Thad, what have you done?"* Cleo whispered, the gravity of the situation sinking in like the weight of a bad decision.

But the mystery was far from solved. How had Acme's competitors gained access to this information? Cleo knew that AI models like CHATTERBOTGPT were complex and far-reaching, their outputs the result of countless data inputs from around the globe. If Thad's uploads had been used as training data, then it was possible-- no, likely-- that the AI had repurposed this data, weaving it into the very strategies now being celebrated by Acme's rivals.

Cleo's thoughts then turned to research a comforting ally in the uncertain landscape of corporate intrigue. She decided to dig deeper into the scientific literature surrounding CHATTERBOTGPT, hoping to uncover any hidden dangers lurking behind its polished facade. And so, armed with her laptop and an insatiable curiosity, Cleo delved into the world of academic papers, technical reports, and research articles.

The papers she found were both enlightening and alarming. CHATTERBOTGPT, it seemed, was not as innocuous as its promoters made it out to be. The AI's data management practices were far more complex than Thad, or anyone at Acme, had realized. The research revealed how the AI processed vast amounts of data, repurposing it in ways that were both unforeseen and uncontrollable. There were mentions of unforeseen risks, potential data leaks, unintended biases, and the dangers of over-reliance on AI-generated content. These warnings were often buried in footnotes or glossed over entirely.

As Cleo absorbed this information, a picture began to form, a picture of an AI that was not only powerful but dangerously unpredictable. It was clear now that the competitors weren't just benefiting from AI-generated content; they were unknowingly drawing from a well tainted with Acme's most prized secrets.

Her thoughts returned to The Daily Grind, where she had overheard those unsettling conversations. The assistants from rival companies had practically crowed about how their AIs were making them look like geniuses. Could it be that they were unwittingly benefiting from Thad's reckless data dump? The pieces of the puzzle were falling into place, but the picture they formed was anything but reassuring.

Determined to uncover the full extent of the leak, Cleo decided to reach out to her network of contacts across Sillycon Valley. Over the years, she had cultivated relationships with key players, people who owed her favors, or who simply couldn't resist a good chat. Disguising her inquiries as casual conversation, Cleo began to gather intel, asking subtle questions about the latest AI tools and any peculiar coincidences her contacts might have noticed.

What she learned was as enlightening as it was alarming. Several of her contacts mentioned how their companies had recently adopted CHATTERBOTGPT, each one raving about the tool's uncanny ability to generate insights that seemed almost too perfect. None of them realized that these insights were the result of Acme's secrets being repurposed and distributed by the AI.

Cleo's heart raced as the full scope of the situation became clear. The competitors weren't just benefiting from AI-generated content; they were using Acme's own data to outmaneuver the very company that had created it. And the worst part? None of them, not even Thad, had any idea of the true source of their newfound brilliance.

With this revelation, Cleo knew she was closer to the truth than ever before, but the situation was far from resolved. She needed irrefutable proof, evidence that would protect Acme and salvage what was left of its competitive edge.

And so, dear reader, our tale continues, with Cleo at the helm of a corporate sleuthing mission that promises to uncover hidden connections and protect Acme from the storm that is now looming on the horizon.

## The Gathering Storm

The atmosphere at Acme Inc. had shifted. What once felt like a whirlwind of excitement now carried an undercurrent of unease, the kind that makes one glance over their shoulder without knowing why. Thaddeus Blandly, basking in the rare warmth of Edison Sparks' approval, should have felt triumphant. But instead, a weed of doubt had begun to sprout in the fertile soil of his mind. It started with a look, a fleeting glance from Cleo Catchall, whose usually bright eyes had dimmed ever so slightly, like a light bulb on the verge of flickering out. It wasn't a look of disdain or disappointment; no, it was something far more troubling: *concern*. And Thad, for all his obliviousness, couldn't ignore it.

As the day wore on, that concern continued taking root in Thad's mind. He replayed the events of the past few days in his head, his hurried uploads to CHATTERBOTGPT, the lavish praise from Sparks, the momentary glory of being the company's unexpected hero. But now, standing in the middle of his cubicle, Thad began to wonder if he had, in fact, been too hasty, too eager to embrace the magic of artificial intelligence without truly understanding its consequences.

The final straw came during his afternoon visit to The Daily Grind, where Thad had gone to clear his mind with a cup of coffee and one of his cherished fortune cookies. As he waited for his order, his ears perked up at a conversation happening at the next table. Two executive assistants from a rival company were chatting, their voices carrying just enough for Thad to catch snippets of their exchange.

*"Our AI is amazing!"* one of them gushed. *"We've got this new widget design that's going to blow Acme out*

*of the water. It's like we've got a crystal ball, predicting exactly what the market needs."*

The other executive assistant laughed, adding, *"Yeah, it's like we've tapped into Acme's secret sauce! They won't know what hit them."*

Thad froze, his heart skipping a beat. The words echoed in his mind, mingling with the growing anxiety he had been trying to suppress. How could they know about Acme's designs? The uncanny resemblance to Acme's projects couldn't be a coincidence, could it? Thad's mind raced, connecting dots he desperately hoped didn't belong together.

*"What if..."* Thad whispered to himself, the question trailing off into the ether as his mind wandered down a dark and twisting path. What if the very tool that had brought him acclaim was also the harbinger of Acme's downfall?

Back at his desk, his hand, almost of its own accord, reached into the drawer where he kept his collection of fortune cookies, his secret comfort in times of uncertainty. Today, he needed reassurance more than ever. He cracked open the first cookie, the satisfying snap echoing in the quiet of his cubicle. The fortune inside read:

---

*YOUR HARD WORK WILL*
*SOON*
*PAY OFF.*

---

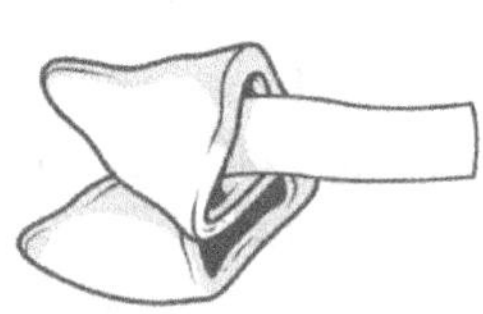

Thad exhaled a breath he didn't realize he was holding. Perhaps this was all just in his mind, an overreaction born of stress and self-doubt. Surely, his climb to the top was inevitable, and this nagging feeling of impending doom was nothing more than a passing cloud.

But the doubt remained, gnawing at the edges of his consciousness. So, Thad reached for another cookie. This time, the fortune was less comforting:

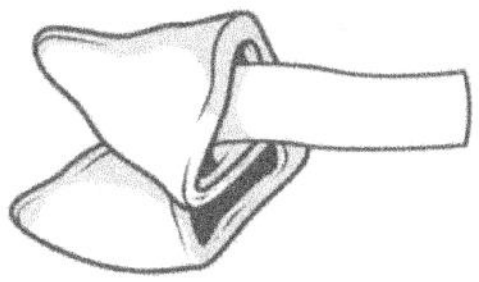

*BEWARE OF FALSE FRIENDS.*

Thad's heart skipped a beat. Could this be a sign? Was there someone within Acme who couldn't be trusted? His thoughts flickered to Cleo, then quickly darted away; no, it couldn't be her. She was the glue that held the company together, the one person who had always looked out for him. The cookies offered no real solace, only more questions, and as Thad cracked open cookie after cookie, the fortunes became increasingly cryptic, as if they were taunting him with the ambiguity of fate.

---

*THE PATH TO SUCCESS IS NOT ALWAYS CLEAR.*

*WHAT YOU SEEK IS WITHIN REACH, BUT AT WHAT COST?*

*TRUST YOUR INSTINCTS, BUT DO NOT IGNORE THE SIGNS.*

---

By the time Thad reached the bottom of the cookie drawer, he was more unsettled than ever. He began to wonder if the fortunes were reflecting the turmoil in his own mind, a mind that was now teetering on the edge of panic. He needed to know the truth, to confirm that his fears were unfounded and that everything was, indeed, under control.

Across the office, Cleo was in full sleuth mode, her mind whirring with the speed of a supercomputer as she pieced together the puzzle that had been plaguing her since The Daily Grind. The more she uncovered, the more urgent the situation seemed. With each new discovery, the storm clouds gathered, darkening the horizon with the threat of an impending catastrophe.

Cleo had spent days poring over logs and files, diving deep into the scientific research she had unearthed. What she found was nothing short of alarming: CHATTERBOTGPT, while powerful, was a ticking time bomb of unintended consequences. The AI's data management practices were, in a word, unpredictable. It repurposed information in ways that were as creative as they were dangerous, blending Acme's secrets into outputs that could be accessed by anyone who happened to stumble upon them. And stumble upon them they had.

Cleo's suspicions were confirmed when she discovered that one of Acme's fiercest competitors, Innovatech Corp., was preparing to unveil a new line of widgets, one that bore an uncanny resemblance to Acme's most top-secret project. The realization hit her like a cold splash of water to the face. Innovatech had Acme's blueprints, and they were planning to use them to leapfrog ahead in the market. Her pulse quickened as she connected the dots.

Thad's uploads to CHATTERBOTGPT had been more than just a careless act; they had been an open invitation for Acme's rivals to siphon off its innovations. And now, the repercussions of that mistake were thundering toward them. But there was no time for panic, no time to dwell on the what-ifs. Cleo was nothing if not a woman of action, and she knew that if Acme had any hope of weathering this storm, she needed to act fast. The clock was ticking, and every second brought their competitors closer to the finish line.

That night, as the office emptied out and the fluorescent lights cast long shadows across the walls, Cleo remained at her desk, her fingers flying over the keyboard. She reached out to Jessup once more, this time with a different request: to help her scrub any trace of the sensitive data from Acme's network and to implement additional security measures. She couldn't undo what had been done, but she could at least try to prevent further leaks.

Meanwhile, Thad, unable to shake the growing sense of dread, decided to do a bit of investigating of his own. He retraced his steps, checking the logs and reviewing the files he had uploaded. The more he looked, the more his stomach churned. It wasn't just the sheer volume of data he had shared; it was the realization that he had done so with almost no safeguards in place. *"This can't be good,"* Thad muttered, his earlier bravado evaporating like morning dew under the harsh light of day.

As the night wore on, Cleo and Thad's paths converged. The two of them, driven by a shared desire to protect Acme, found themselves the next morning standing outside Edison Sparks' office, each holding a stack of evidence that pointed to the same grim conclusion: Acme's future was in jeopardy, and they were running out of time to save it. But before they could knock on the door, Cleo stopped Thad with a gentle hand on his arm. *"We need to be sure,"* she whispered, her voice steady but laced with urgency. *"If we go in there with half-truths, we'll only make things worse."* Thad nodded, the gravity of the situation sinking in. He didn't have the answers, and that terrified him. But he trusted Cleo. He always had, and he knew that if anyone could navigate them through this storm, it was her.

And so, dear reader, our tale reaches a critical juncture. Cleo and Thad stand on the precipice of a revelation that could either save Acme or doom it to a fate none of them had foreseen. The gathering storm is about to break, and with it, the truth will come to light, whether they're ready for it or not.

## Dr. A's Reflections

Here we are, dear reader, standing on the brink of a revelation. It is imperative that we pause and consider the gravity of what has transpired. The path we've traveled so far, lined with the glittering promise of technological wonders, has led us to a precipice where innovation teeters on the edge of disaster. The events at Acme Inc., driven by ambition and, dare I say, a touch of hubris, serve as a stark reminder that in the race to innovate, reflection is often the first casualty.

Thaddeus Blandly, our well-meaning but ill-prepared protagonist, is learning this lesson the hard way. His eager embrace of artificial intelligence, a tool he believed would catapult him to success, has instead become a double-edged sword. As the winds of consequence begin to howl, Thad finds himself at the mercy of forces he barely understands, forces that threaten to unravel not just his efforts, but the very fabric of Acme's future.

And then there is Cleo Catchall, the steady hand in this maelstrom of innovation gone awry. Cleo, with her sharp instincts and unyielding resolve, is acutely aware that the stakes have never been higher. She knows that the brilliance of invention is not enough; it must be tempered with caution, with foresight, with an understanding that every shortcut carries a hidden cost. The choices she makes in the coming moments will determine whether Acme survives this storm or is swept away by it.

As I observe the unfolding events, I am reminded of a truth that is as old as time itself: innovation without wisdom is a recipe for disaster. It is not enough to have the tools, the technology, or even the knowledge; one must also possess the discernment to use them wisely. For in the world of innovation, as in life, there are no guarantees, no sure paths to success. There are only choices, and the consequences that follow.

Our story, dear reader, is far from over. The choices made by Thad, Cleo, and the others will soon converge, and the true test of their resolve will begin. But for now, let us take this moment to reflect on the lessons we have learned: that innovation is a journey, not a destination; that shortcuts often lead to unforeseen perils; and that the true measure of success lies not in what we achieve, but in how we navigate the challenges along the way.

And so, dear reader, as we prepare to rejoin our intrepid characters on their journey, remember that innovation, like life, is full of surprises-- some delightful, others less so. But it is in these moments of uncertainty that true character is revealed, and it is in these moments that our story will find its heart.

## Unraveling the Web

The door to Edison Sparks' office loomed before Cleo and Thad like the entrance to a vault holding the company's most precious secrets. But neither of them was ready to enter just yet. The weight of the evidence in their hands felt like a ticking clock, counting down to a moment they could not yet fully grasp. Cleo's hand lingered on Thad's arm, her eyes filled with determination and a hint of something else, something like fear.

*"Thad,"* she began, her voice a soft whisper in the dim hallway, *"before we go in, we need to understand the full scope of what's happened. We can't go to Sparks with anything less than the truth, the whole truth."*

Thad nodded, his mind swirling with the implications of what he had overheard at The Daily Grind, what he had seen in the logs, and what he now knew to be true. The storm that had been brewing was no longer just a metaphor; it was real, and its winds were already tearing through the foundations of Acme Inc.

The two retreated to the small conference room they had occupied earlier, the evidence laid out before them like pieces of a complex puzzle, one they had no choice but to solve.

Cleo took a deep breath, her fingers once again flying over the keyboard as she pulled up more data, more connections, more clues.

*"Let's start with Innovatech,"* Cleo said, her voice steady despite the anxiety simmering beneath the surface. *"They're the ones closest to launching a widget based on what they've gleaned from ChatterBotGPT. But they're not the only ones. I've*

*found traces of our designs, our strategies, even our marketing plans in the hands of at least two other competitors. It's as if we've been feeding them our playbook without even realizing it."*

Thad's heart sank further with each word. The reality of what he had done; the ease with which he had handed over Acme's secrets to an AI that was anything but secure; hit him like a freight train. *"I never thought... I didn't realize it could do this,"* he murmured, his voice filled with regret. *"I just wanted to help, to show that I could contribute something valuable."*

Cleo paused, her gaze softening as she looked at Thad. *"I know you did, Thad. And in another world, maybe this could have been a breakthrough. But the way things stand now... we're facing a full-scale crisis. If Innovatech and the others go public with what they've developed, it'll be the end of Acme's competitive edge."*

Thad swallowed hard, the taste of fear bitter on his tongue. *"So what do we do?"* he asked, desperate for a solution, for some way to undo the damage he had caused.

*"We need to contain this as much as we can,"* Cleo replied, her mind already several steps ahead. *"Jessup's working on scrubbing our network, but we also need to figure out how to deal with the data that's already out there. Maybe we can delay Innovatech's launch or find a way to prove that what they're using isn't entirely theirs. But first, we have to be honest with Sparks. He needs to know exactly what's happened and what we're up against."*

Thad nodded, feeling the full weight of his responsibility settle on his shoulders. For once, there were no fortune cookies to guide him, no cryptic messages to offer reassurance. This was real, and it was happening now. "*Okay,*" he said, his voice trembling slightly but gaining strength as he spoke. *"Let's do it. Let's figure this out."*

*"This is bigger than just a leak,"* Cleo said at one point, her voice tinged with disbelief. *"It's like we've opened Pandora's box, and now we have to figure out how to close it before it's too late."* Thad looked at her, a flicker of hope in his eyes. *"But we can close it, right? We can still fix this. right?"* Cleo met his gaze, her expression resolute. *"We have to try, Thad. For Acme's sake, we have to try."*

As the hours ticked by, they compiled their findings into a coherent narrative, a story of ambition, innovation, and unintended consequences that had led Acme to the brink of disaster. It was a story that needed to be told, not just to Sparks, but to everyone who had placed their trust in the technology that was now unraveling before them.

And so, with the evidence in hand and a plan beginning to take shape, Cleo and Thad finally stood up, ready to face the storm that was now fully upon them. The door to Edison Sparks' office no longer seemed as ominous as it had before, but the gravity of what lay ahead was undeniable.

.

## Chapter Summary

As Thad continues to bask in his perceived brilliance, Cleo Catchall begins uncovering troubling patterns. Conversations at The Daily Grind and her meticulous detective work lead her to discover the true extent of the consequences stemming from Thad's actions. The chapter delves into Cleo's role as the unsung hero and the growing tension as Acme's competitors unknowingly benefit from their secret data.

### Key Takeaways

- Vigilance and skepticism are critical when dealing with technology in high-stakes environments.
- Oversight in data handling can lead to unintended consequences across an organization and industry.
- The unsung efforts of individuals like Cleo often determine the success or failure of an organization during a crisis.

## Reflection Exercise

Cleo demonstrates the importance of curiosity and initiative in uncovering risks. Describe a time when taking initiative helped solve a problem or uncover a hidden issue in your life or work.

## Critical Thinking Questions

1. Cleo uncovers the problem by paying attention to small details and informal conversations. How can companies encourage employees to speak up when they notice something suspicious?

2. Thad's actions indirectly benefit Acme's

competitors. How can organizations mitigate risks when sharing or using sensitive information with AI tools?

3. Reflect on Cleo's investigative approach. What qualities made her successful in uncovering the

truth, and how can you apply those qualities in your work or personal projects?

______________________________________________

______________________________________________

______________________________________________

## Practical Applications

**Build a *"Red Flags"* Checklist:** Create a list of indicators that might suggest misuse of data or technology within your workplace or organization.

______________________________________________

______________________________________________

______________________________________________

______________________________________________

______________________________________________

**Role-Playing Exercise**: Imagine you are Cleo investigating a potential data breach. How would you approach finding evidence and escalating the issue?

**Personal Audit**: Review how you handle sensitive data in your daily activities. Identify one improvement you can make to increase security.

## Your Notes

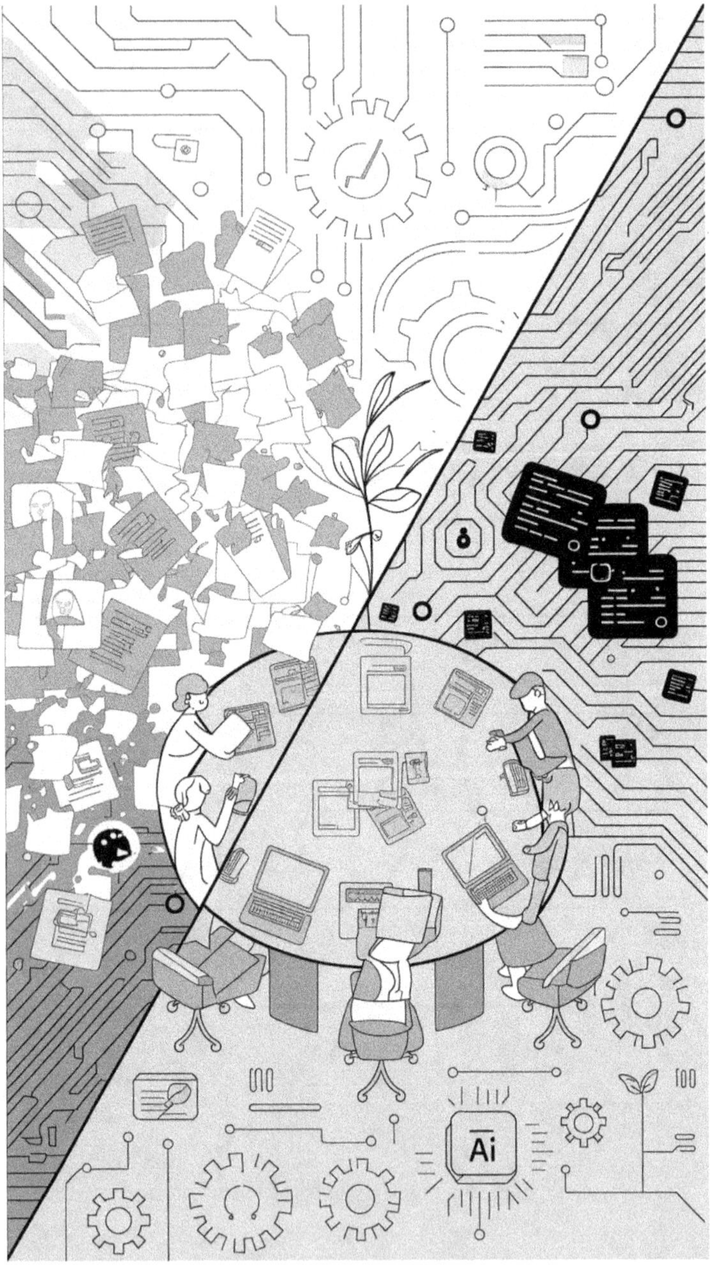
Ai

# Chapter III

## Confrontation in the Boardroom

The atmosphere in the boardroom was thick with tension, the kind that seems to seep into the walls and settle into the very air you breathe. Cleo and Thad sat at one end of the long, polished table, the weight of the documents and data they had gathered pressing heavily on them. At the other end, Edison Sparks paced back and forth, his usual buoyant energy now tinged with an edge of anxiety.
*"Alright,"* Sparks said, finally coming to a stop and fixing Cleo and Thad with an expectant gaze. *"Tell me what we're dealing with."*

Cleo took a deep breath and began, her voice steady but laced with urgency. *"We've confirmed that Innovatech Corp. and at least two other competitors have gained access to our proprietary designs and strategies through the data Thad uploaded to ChatterBotGPT. They've integrated these insights into their upcoming widget launches, the first of which is Innovatech's, scheduled for the end of this week."*

Sparks' eyes narrowed as he absorbed the information. *"How bad is it?" "It's bad,"* Thad said, his voice tinged with guilt. *"The widget Innovatech is about to launch... it's almost a carbon copy of our latest top-secret project. If they go public with it before we do, they'll beat us to market, and it'll look like we're the ones copying them."* Sparks let out a low whistle, the gravity of the situation sinking in. *"So, what are our options?"* Cleo leaned forward, spreading out a series of documents on the table. *"We've identified a few possible counterstrategies, but each comes with its own risks and potential drawbacks."*

She pointed to the first document. *"Option one: We could file for an immediate injunction to stop*

*Innovatech from launching their widget. The advantage here is that it buys us timeto regroup, to solidify our position, and to prevent Innovatech from stealing our thunder. But the downside is that it could backfire. If the court denies our request or if Innovatech argues that their designs are sufficiently different, we could end up looking desperate, even paranoid. Worse, we might have to reveal more of our own work to make the case, which could expose us even further.'*Sparks nodded, considering the implications. *"And if we go that route, it's a public move. The media would catch wind of it, and it could shake investor confidence."*

*"Exactly,"* Cleo agreed. *"Option two: We could launch a counter-campaign, rush our widget to market ahead of Innovatech's launch, even if it means cutting corners on the final touches. The benefit is that we stay ahead of the curve and maintain our image as industry leaders. However, the risks are significant. If we launch before we're fully ready, the widget might have flaws or underdeliver on expectations. That could damage our reputation and result in long-term losses."* Thad shifted uncomfortably in his seat. *"Plus, there's the added pressure on our teams. They're already stretched thin and pushing them harder could lead to burnout or mistakes that we can't afford."* Sparks drummed his fingers on the table, deep in thought. *"Alright, what's the third option?"*

*"The third option,"* Cleo continued, *"is to go public with what's happened, acknowledge the breach and position ourselves as the victims of industrial espionage. We could frame it as a warning to the industry about the dangers of misused AI and data security lapses. This approach might generate sympathy and buy us time to regroup. But it's not without risk. We'd be exposing our vulnerabilities, admitting to a significant oversight, and potentially*

*inviting scrutiny from regulators, competitors, and the public."*

Sparks looked at Thad with practiced empathy. *"And we'd be putting Thad in the spotlight,"* Sparks added, glancing at Thad, who looked like he'd rather be anywhere but there. *"The media would eat this up--and not in a good way."* Thad swallowed hard. *"I know I messed up, but if coming clean is what it takes to fix this, I'm willing to do it."* Sparks sighed, running a hand through his hair. *"These are all risky moves. Is there any way we can combine them? File the injunction while preparing for a quick launch, and then decide on the PR strategy depending on how the first two play out?"* Cleo considered it. *"It's possible, but it would require a coordinated effort on all fronts. We'd need our legal team to move fast, our engineers to work around the clock, and our PR department to be ready with a response, whatever the outcome."*

*"Coordinated chaos,"* Sparks muttered, pacing again. *"But it might be our best shot."* The room fell into a contemplative silence as each person considered the options before them. The stakes were high, and the wrong move could spell disaster for Acme Inc. But doing nothing wasn't an option either. Finally, Sparks stopped pacing and turned to face Cleo and Thad, his expression resolute. *"Alright. We'll go with the coordinated approach. Cleo, you work with Jessup and the engineers to prepare for an accelerated launch. Thad, I need you to work with legal on the injunction and then be ready to assist PR if we have to go public. We're all in this together, and if we're going to weather this storm, we need to be united."*

Cleo and Thad nodded. The clock was ticking, and the next few days would determine the fate of Acme Inc. As they left the boardroom, each carrying the burden of their tasks, the sense of urgency was palpable. All they could do now was hope that their efforts would be enough to keep Acme afloat in the raging waters of competition and crisis.

## The Last Ditch Effort

The clock in Cleo Catchall's office ticked with an ominous regularity, each second a stark reminder of the precious time slipping away. Normally, Acme Inc. bustled with energy, a hive of innovation and creativity. But tonight, it was eerily quiet. The usual hum of laughter and conversation was replaced by the low drone of computers, the hurried clicks of keyboards, and the muffled voices of those who, like Cleo, were still desperately working against the clock. The stakes had never been higher, and everyone knew it, but for Cleo, the pressure felt particularly suffocating. As she sat at her desk, the glow of her monitor casting sharp shadows across her face, Cleo felt the future of the entire company pressing down on her shoulders. Her eyes darted over the screen, scanning a dizzying array of data-- project timelines, security protocols, legal documents-- each one a piece of the intricate puzzle they were scrambling to fit together.

The coordinated approach was in full swing, but the margin for error was paper-thin. One misstep, one overlooked detail, and everything could come crashing down. Cleo's mind raced, trying to stay a step ahead of the chaos. She was known for her quick thinking and sharp instincts, but tonight, doubt gnawed at the edges of her resolve. What if they had missed something? What if the security measures weren't enough or the injunction fell through? The thought of Acme's competitors unveiling their stolen innovations made her stomach churn with anxiety. She had always prided herself on being the glue that held Acme together, the steady hand guiding the company through its most challenging moments. But now, as the enormity of their situation unfolded, Cleo felt the creeping tendrils of fear wrap around her. This wasn't just another tough project; this was a crisis that could define her career and possibly end Acme Inc.

Cleo found herself questioning everything. Had they done enough? Were they moving fast enough? Was there some crucial element she had overlooked in the frenzy of the past few hours? And beneath it all, a deeper, more personal concern gnawed at her: the fear of failure. Cleo had always been driven by a need to prove herself, to show that she could thrive in an industry that so often underestimated her. But tonight, the fear that she might not be able to pull them through this crisis, that she might let everyone down, was almost paralyzing. There was no time to dwell on those fears. Cleo pushed them aside, focusing on the task at hand.

Across the office, Jessup, the company's IT savant, was frantically typing away, his fingers flying over the keyboard with a speed that defied belief. His usual laid-back demeanor had been replaced with a laser focus. They were implementing new security measures, locking down Acme's network with a level of rigor usually reserved for state secrets. Every file, every email, every digital footprint was being scrutinized, cleaned, and fortified against further breaches.

*"Jessup, how's it looking?"* Cleo called out, her voice tinged with urgency. *"Better than it was an hour ago,"* Jessup replied without looking up. *"I've got the firewall up and running at full capacity. I've added a new pop-up warning message that displays when employees go to access ChatterBotGPT - letting them know not to upload any confidential data."* Cleo

nodded, acknowledging the grim reality. *"Keep at it. We can't afford any more surprises."*

Meanwhile, Thad was in a meeting with Acme's legal team, the room filled with the hushed tones of intense discussion. The legal team, a group of sharp-eyed attorneys with years of experience navigating corporate legal battles, was poring over the documents Cleo and Thad had presented, weighing the risks and benefits of filing for an injunction against Innovatech. Thad sat stiffly in his chair, feeling out of place among the seasoned attorneys, but determined to see this through.

*"Thad, we need you to confirm exactly what files were uploaded to ChatterBotGPT,"* one of the attorneys said, her tone clipped and professional. *"We need to make sure we have enough evidence to justify an injunction. If Innovatech pushes back, we need to be able to prove that they're using our proprietary information."*

Thad swallowed hard, his mind racing as he tried to recall every detail. *"I-- I uploaded design documents, project notes, strategy briefs... pretty much everything related to the new widget line we were developing. I thought it would help refine the outputs..."*

The attorney nodded, making notes. *"Alright. We'll draft the injunction and submit it first thing in the morning. But you need to be prepared; if this goes to court, you'll be called to testify. We need you to be clear and concise about what happened."*

Another attorney, older and with a more cautious demeanor, leaned back in his chair, his brow furrowed in thought. *"An injunction is a bold move, but it's also risky. Innovatech is likely to fight back, and we'll need ironclad proof that they've used our proprietary information. If we can't provide that, or if the judge perceives our case as weak, we could end up doing more harm than good."*

The lead attorney, a woman known for her strategic mind, nodded in agreement. "There's also the issue of timing. An injunction could delay Innovatech's launch, but it's a temporary solution. If we don't have a long-term strategy to protect our intellectual property, we'll be vulnerable as soon as the injunction is lifted."

Thad shifted uncomfortably. "*So, what are our other options? Is there something else we can do?*" The cautious attorney spoke up again. "*One alternative might be to file for a declaratory judgment instead. This would allow us to assert our rights without immediately seeking to block Innovatech's launch. It's less aggressive than an injunction and could buy us time to gather more evidence or negotiate a settlement. However, it also means that Innovatech could proceed with their launch while the case is being decided, which is a risk."*

The lead attorney considered this, then added, "Another avenue worth exploring, though decidedly unglamorous, is the trade secrets angle. Should we manage to demonstrate that Innovatech is utilizing information that qualifies under the Uniform Trade Secrets Act, we could pursue legal action. This might grant us a modicum of leverage in negotiations and, if successful, secure stronger and more enforceable protections—though I wouldn't suggest holding your breath for a cinematic courtroom finale."

"*But,*" she continued, "*going down the trade secrets route requires us to clearly define what constitutes a trade secret and prove that Innovatech acquired it improperly. It's a tougher case to make, but it could be more effective in the long run.*" Thad listened intently, trying to absorb the legal intricacies being discussed. He wasn't a lawyer, but he understood the gravity of the situation. *"What do you think is our best shot?"* he asked, his voice steady despite the tension. The lead attorney leaned forward, folding her hands on the table. *"Filing for an injunction is still our strongest immediate move if we want to stop Innovatech in their tracks, but we need to be prepared for a fight. If we can back it up with a trade secrets claim or a declaratory judgment as a fallback, we'll have more options depending on how Innovatech responds."*

She paused, her gaze piercing. *"Thad, if we go down this path, you need to be prepared for the possibility that this could turn into a drawn-out legal battle. Innovatech isn't going to roll over easily, and this could get messy. Are you ready for that?"* Thad nodded, the weight of the situation pressing down on him, but his resolve was clear. *"I'll do whatever it takes. I messed up, and I'm ready to face the consequences, whatever they are."* The room fell silent for a moment as the attorneys considered their next steps.

Finally, the lead attorney spoke again, her voice firm. *"Alright. We'll proceed with the injunction, but we'll also prepare the groundwork for a trade secrets claim and explore the possibility of a declaratory judgment. We need to cover all our bases."* The team nodded in agreement, and Thad felt a surge of determination. There was no turning back now; they were all in, and the battle to protect Acme's future was about to begin. The path ahead was fraught with uncertainty, but Thad was determined to see it through, no matter the cost.

Back in the office, Cleo was coordinating with the engineering team, who were working around the clock to prepare for an accelerated launch of Acme's own widget. The atmosphere was tense, the pressure palpable. They were cutting corners, pushing the limits of what was possible, but there was no other choice. It was a race against time, and Innovatech was already miles ahead.

*"Cleo, we're hitting roadblocks with the final testing,"* one of the lead engineers said, his voice strained with exhaustion. *"If we push this too fast, we risk rolling out a widget that isn't fully vetted. We could end up with glitches, or worse, a complete failure."* Cleo pressed her fingers to her temples, feeling the stress pounding at her skull. *"I know it's risky, but we don't have the luxury of time. Do what you can, prioritize the most critical functions, and we'll deal with the rest later. We just need to get something out there before Innovatech does." The engineer nodded, though his expression remained grim. "We'll do our best."*

As the night wore on, the office buzzed with the frenetic energy of a team on the edge. Every department was working in overdrive-- legal, engineering, PR-- all trying to stave off the impending disaster. Cleo coordinated each moving part with the precision of a conductor leading an orchestra, though she knew the symphony they were playing was far from harmonious.

Thad, feeling restless after his meeting, wandered through the halls, his mind a blur of anxiety and regret. The reality of what they were facing was overwhelming, and he couldn't shake the feeling that it was all his fault. He found himself in the break room, staring at the vending machine, considering whether another fortune cookie might offer some form of solace. But he knew better now. The answers weren't in the cookies; they were in the hard work and decisions that lay ahead.

Returning to Cleo's office, Thad found her still at her desk, surrounded by papers and glowing screens. She looked up as he entered, offering him a weary smile. *"How's it going?"* Thad asked, though he could see the strain in her eyes. *"About as well as can be expected,"* Cleo replied. *"We're making progress, but it's touch and go. How did it go with legal?"*

*"They're filing the injunction in the morning,"* Thad said, taking a seat opposite her. *"But it's a gamble. If Innovatech fights it, we might be in for a long, ugly battle."* Cleo nodded, her gaze distant as she considered the implications. *"We're doing everything we can, Thad. We just have to hope it's enough."* The two sat in silence for a moment, the enormity of the situation hanging heavily between them. Finally, Cleo spoke again, her voice softer now. *"We'll get through this,"* she said, more to herself than to him. *"We have to."* Thad nodded, though the uncertainty in his heart was hard to shake. *"Yeah. We have to."*

As the first light of dawn began to creep through the windows, Cleo and Thad knew that the hours ahead would be some of the most challenging of their careers. The last-ditch effort was in full swing. All they could do now was give it everything they had, and hope that, somehow, it would be enough to weather the storm.

## Dr A's Commentary

Ah, dear reader, it is I again, Dr. A, your ever-watchful narrator, returning to you at this pivotal juncture in our tale. We find ourselves on the cusp of what promises to be a storm of epic proportions, where the forces of innovation and the consequences of human error are about to collide in a most dramatic fashion. But before the winds of fate sweep us further into the maelstrom, let us take a moment to pause, to reflect, and to consider the delicate dance that is crisis management in the world of technology.

At the frontier of innovation, time is both an ally and an enemy. It is the ticking clock that drives us forward, urging us to seize opportunities before they slip through our fingers. But it is also the relentless force that can turn even the best-laid plans to dust if we are not careful. The pressure of last-minute efforts, the frantic scramble to stay ahead of the competition, can often lead us to make decisions in haste-- decisions that, while well-intentioned, may ultimately lead us down a path fraught with peril.

Our friends, Cleo, Thad, and Sparks, find themselves in just such a pickle. The stakes are impossibly high, and the margin for error is vanishingly small. Every second that passes brings them closer to the moment of truth, when the results of their efforts will be laid bare for all to see. It is a time of tension, of anticipation, of knowing that the choices they make now will determine not only their own fates but the fate of Acme Inc. as a whole.

Crisis management, you see, is not just about solving problems; it is about navigating the treacherous waters of uncertainty with a steady hand and a clear mind. It is about making the right decisions when every option carries its own risks and rewards, about balancing the need for swift action with the importance of careful deliberation. It is a test of character, of resilience, and, above all, of wisdom.

In this calm before the storm, we must also consider the thin line that separates success from failure in the world of innovation. That line is often so fine as to be invisible, yet it is there, waiting to catch the unwary. One misjudged move, and the entire edifice of success can come crashing down. Yet, on the other side of that line lies the potential for greatness, the chance to turn a crisis into an opportunity, to emerge from the storm stronger and more capable than before.

As we prepare to step into the next chapter of our story, let us remember that innovation is not just about the pursuit of new ideas; it is about the courage to face the unknown, the wisdom to learn from our mistakes, and the strength to carry on when the odds are stacked against us. Cleo, Thad, and Sparks are about to face their greatest challenge yet, and the outcome is anything but certain.

So, dear reader, take a deep breath. The calm we have experienced is but a fleeting moment, a brief respite before the forces of innovation and crisis collide. And when they do, we will see just how thin that line between success and failure truly is.

Until then, I remain your ever-faithful guide, Dr. A.

## Chapter Summary

The storm comes to a head as Cleo and Thad confront Edison Sparks with the truth about Acme's data leak. The team faces tough decisions: legal action, rushed widget launches, or public transparency. Each choice carries its own risks, and the urgency to act tests the company's resilience and teamwork.

### Key Takeaways

Crisis management requires clear communication, quick decision-making, and collaboration.

The decisions made during a crisis can have long-term consequences for a company's reputation and stability.

Transparency and accountability are crucial in rebuilding trust after a crisis.

### Reflection Exercise

Crisis moments often reveal character and values. When was a time when you had to make a difficult decision under

## Critical Thinking Questions

1. Acme's leadership debates how to respond to Innovatech's launch. What are the pros and cons of their

2. How does Cleo's calm and methodical approach contrast with Thad's impulsiveness? What lessons can be learned from their different responses?

3. What role does leadership play in guiding a team through a crisis, and how can leaders like Sparks balance urgency with strategic thinking?

## Practical Applications

**Crisis Response Plan**: Draft a mock crisis response plan for a hypothetical data breach. Include legal, operational, and communication strategies.

| Plan | Scenario 1 | Scenario 2 |
|---|---|---|
| Trigger | | |
| Crisis Management Team Members called to action | | |
| Action to be taken | | |

**Decision Matrix**: Create a decision matrix for evaluating responses to crises. Use Acme's situation as an example to weigh risks and benefit: Low: 1, Medium: 2, High: 3)

| OPTIONS | COST | RISK | SPEED | REPUTA-TION | Total |
|---|---|---|---|---|---|
| File Injunction | | | | | |
| Rush product launch | | | | | |
| Go public with the breach | | | | | |

**Role-Playing Exercise**: Split into teams to simulate a boardroom crisis discussion. Assign roles like CEO, legal counsel, and technical lead. Present solutions and debate their viability.

**Boardroom Crisis Scenario**: Your company, AIWorks, has released a generative AI tool called QuickDraft, designed to help businesses create marketing content. The tool has been praised for its ease of use and creativity but recently came under fire when a journalist discovered it generates biased and offensive content when prompted with certain terms. The issue has gone viral on social media, with customers, investors, and the media demanding answers. The leadership team must convene to decide how to handle the immediate backlash and ensure this issue does not happen again.

Roles:

**CEO**: Focused on protecting the company's reputation and guiding the team toward a solution that balances short-term damage control with long-term goals.

**Chief Technology Officer (CTO)**: Explains how the bias may have entered the AI model and proposes technical solutions to address it.

**Head of PR and Marketing**: Focuses on controlling the narrative, drafting public statements, and addressing customer concerns to rebuild trust.

**Legal Counsel:** Considers the regulatory and legal implications, including the risk of lawsuits or compliance violations.

**Ethics Officer:** Evaluates the ethical dimensions of the issue, including how bias affects different user groups and what steps can be taken to prevent harm.

**Product Manager**: Analyzes how fixing the issue will impact product timelines, customer satisfaction, and competitive positioning.

Debrief Questions:

1. How did the team balance technical fixes with public-facing responses?
2. What was the most challenging conflict to resolve during the discussion?
3. How would the proposed solution affect the company's reputation, both short- and long-term?

## Your Notes

# Chapter IV

## The Unveiling

The day had arrived. Innovatech's much-anticipated widget launch was set to take place in the heart of Sillycon Valley, the epicenter of technological ambition. The venue was a gleaming glass-and-steel auditorium, its modern design reflecting the cutting-edge innovations it housed. The atmosphere inside was electric, charged with the palpable anticipation of the industry's most influential players, all eager to witness the unveiling of what promised to be a game-changing widget.

Among the crowd sat Acme Inc.'s delegation, a tight-knit group that included Cleo, Thad, and Sparks. Their expressions were a mix of forced calm and barely concealed anxiety. They had prepared for this moment as best they could, but now that it was here, the uncertainty of what was about to unfold gnawed at each of them.

Cleo's eyes scanned the room, taking in the faces of their competitors, potential partners, and the ever-watchful media. The stakes couldn't be higher. If Innovatech's new widget was indeed based on Acme's proprietary designs, this launch could spell disaster. Her mind raced through the various scenarios, the contingency plans, and the thin sliver of hope they clung to.

Thad, seated beside her, was barely holding it together. The weight of his earlier actions pressed down on him like a leaden blanket. Every fiber of his being screamed for him to do something, but he knew that all he could do now was watch and wait. Sparks, ever the optimist, tried to project confidence, but even he couldn't completely mask the tension in his demeanor. He had been in tight spots before, but this was different. This was personal. This was his company's future on the line.

The lights in the auditorium dimmed, and a hush fell over the crowd as Innovatech's CEO, a sleek and charismatic figure, took the stage. A spotlight followed him as he approached the center, his smile exuding confidence that bordered on smugness. He paused, letting the silence build the suspense before he finally spoke.

*"Ladies and gentlemen, thank you for joining us today. What you're about to see is the culmination of years of hard work, innovation, and a relentless pursuit of excellence. We are proud to present to you the next big leap in technology; the widget that will revolutionize the industry."*

The large screen behind him flickered to life, displaying a sleek animation that gradually morphed into the silhouette of a new widget. The audience leaned forward, captivated by the high-definition visuals that accompanied the CEO's words.

*"As you know,"* the CEO continued, *"Innovatech has always been at the forefront of technological advancement. But this time, we've outdone ourselves. What you're about to see is more than just a widget; it's a vision realized."*

The silhouette on the screen sharpened into focus, revealing the new widget in all its glory. Cleo felt her breath catch in her throat as she recognized the design. It was eerily similar to Acme's top-secret project, the very project Thad had inadvertently exposed through CHATTERBOTGPT.

The Innovatech CEO continued to speak, extolling the virtues of the widget, but Cleo could barely hear him over the pounding of her heart. Thad whispered, his face pale. *"It's our design."* Sparks leaned forward, his eyes narrowing as he scrutinized the screen. *"They stole our design...those fricken, fracken rats."*

The presentation concluded with a flourish, and the room erupted in applause. Innovatech's team looked smug, basking in the praise and admiration being showered upon them. The widget was hailed as a breakthrough, a game-changer that would cement Innovatech's place at the top of the industry.

But while the crowd celebrated, Acme's team sat in stunned silence. They had anticipated something like this, but seeing it unfold in real-time was a gut punch. The sense of betrayal, the frustration, and the overwhelming fear for what this meant for Acme's future hung heavy in the air. Cleo snapped out of her daze and turned to Sparks. *"What do we do? We can't just sit here and let them get away with this."* Sparks clenched his jaw, his mind racing. *"We stick to the plan. We push for the injunction immediately and start preparing our counter-launch. We still have a chance to reclaim this, but we need to move fast."* Thad, still reeling, forced himself to focus. *"And the media? They'll feast on the similarities, demanding to know what it all means, and they won't settle for breadcrumbs.."*

Cleo nodded. *"We need to control the narrative. We can't afford to let Innovatech dominate the story. We need to frame this as what it is: a blatant case of intellectual property theft."* Sparks stood up, his expression hardening into one of determination. *"Then let's go. We're not out of this fight yet."* With that, the team rose, moving swiftly but purposefully out of the auditorium. The battle was far from over. The unveiling had been a blow, but it wasn't the knockout punch Innovatech might have hoped for.

Acme still had cards to play, and they were about to play them with everything they had.

As they exited the building, the cool air outside hit them like cold rain, invigorating their senses. The storm was upon them, but they were ready. The next steps would determine everything.

## The Fallout

The day after the launch, Innovatech's widget was already dominating headlines, with industry insiders hailing it as the next big thing. The media buzzed with excitement, showering Innovatech with praise for their revolutionary innovation. But within the walls of Acme, the mood was anything but celebratory.

Thad Blandly sat at his desk, staring blankly at his computer screen. The news articles flashed before him, each one a painful reminder of what had happened. "INNOVATECH'S NEWEST TRIUMPH!" one headline blared, while another proclaimed, "A GAME-CHANGER IN THE TECH INDUSTRY." The worst of it, though, was the growing suspicion in some corners of the media that Acme had somehow been caught flat-footed, that they were no longer the industry leader they once were.

Thad's mind raced with guilt and regret. This was his fault. He had opened the door to their competitors, and now Acme was paying the price. The voices of doubt and fear that had whispered in the back of his mind for weeks now roared to the forefront, overwhelming him.

Across the office, Cleo Catchall was dealing with the fallout in her own way. She sat in the conference room, papers strewn across the table, her laptop open in front of her as she read through the latest reports. The phone on the table buzzed incessantly with calls from the press, investors, and concerned partners. But Cleo was focused on the task at hand, damage control.

Acme had issued a statement earlier that morning, asserting that they were exploring legal options and that they stood by their commitment to innovation and integrity. But Cleo knew that words alone wouldn't be enough. The press would dig deeper, and Innovatech wasn't going to slow down. Acme was on the back foot, and they needed to find a way to regain their footing.

Sparks entered the room, his usually buoyant energy replaced with a grim determination. *"Give me an update Cleo. The media is going crazy over Innovatech's widget."*

*"We've already filed the injunction,"* Cleo said, *"But we won't see any real results from that for a while, if at all. Innovatech's legal team will fight it, and they're good. We need to focus on our counter-launch, but we're still weeks away from having something ready."* Sparks leaned back in his chair, his mind working through the possibilities. *"And the trade secrets angle?"*

*"It's solid, but it'll take time to build the case. Time we don't have."* Cleo Responded.

Thad appeared in the doorway, hesitating before stepping into the room. Sparks motioned for him to sit down, and Thad did so, his face pale and drawn. *"I'm sorry,"* Thad said quietly, breaking the silence that had settled over the room. *"I didn't mean for any of this to happen. I just wanted to help."* Sparks looked at him, his expression unreadable. *"We know, Thad. But right now, we need to focus on fixing this. Regret isn't going to get us anywhere."*

Thad nodded, though he still couldn't shake the feeling that he had let everyone down. *"What else can I do?"* he asked, his voice filled with a mix of desperation and determination. Cleo exchanged a glance with Sparks before answering. *"Thad, do you remember that master widget idea you presented a few months ago before this all went down? That was a brilliant idea, we just didn't have the resources to work on it." Thad looked pensive for a monent, "Yes I backlogged it."* Cleo brightened *"We need you to revive that project, that may be the one that can help us turn things around."*

Thad felt a flicker of hope. This was his chance to make things right, to atone for the mistake. *"I'll do whatever it takes."* As the three of them discussed their next moves, the tension in the room began to ease, replaced by a renewed sense of purpose. They weren't beaten yet, and if there was one thing Acme had always prided itself on, it was their ability to innovate under pressure.

As the team began to mobilize, Cleo found a moment of quiet in her office. She thought back to the night she had uncovered the full extent of Innovatech's infiltration, the sickening realization that they had been outmaneuvered. But she also remembered the determination that had followed, the resolve to fight back, to protect what they had built. Cleo knew that the road ahead would be difficult, filled with challenges and uncertainty. But she also knew that they had the strength and the resilience to weather the storm.

And so, with the world watching and the clock ticking down, Acme's team prepared to make their stand. The fallout had been severe, but the fight was far from over. They had faced setbacks before, and they had always found a way to come out stronger on the other side. As Cleo closed her laptop and stood up, ready to dive back into the fray, she felt a renewed sense of determination. The stakes were high, but so were the rewards. It was time to show the world what Acme was truly made of.

## Dr. A's Final Reflection

Now, dear reader. the lessons do not end with Thad or Innovatech. Cleo Catchall, ever the diligent and savvy problem-solver, has learned firsthand the need for strategy and governance for AI integration into the business. It was here and it was here to stay. She came to the realization that innovation is as much about responsibility as it is about creativity.

Edison Sparks, the visionary at the helm of Acme Inc., had always treated new technologies like candy in a jar—irresistible and endless. But even candy can rot your teeth. Faced with a series of unwelcome surprises, Edison realized that leading a tech company wasn't just about chasing the next shiny thing. It was a delicate dance: embracing innovation like CHATTERBOTGPT while shoring up the company's bedrock. This meant assessing their AI readiness, patching the cracks, and reigning in rogue tech escapades with governance—a balancing act worthy of any tightrope walker.

The legal storm clouds gathering over Acme Inc. are far from a mere drizzle in their tale of woe. If they march into court against Innovatech, they may discover their legal footing is more quicksand than solid ground. But the trouble doesn't stop at the courthouse steps. Trust, the lifeblood of relationships with stakeholders, investors, and customers, has been rattled like a chandelier in a gale. Meanwhile, the entire industry watches this very public cautionary tale unfold, taking notes on the dangers of leaning too heavily on AI without the safety net of proper safeguards.

So, dear reader, as we prepare to turn the page and move toward the resolution of our story, let us carry forward the lessons learned. Generative AI, for all its brilliance, is not a substitute for human judgment, ethics, or caution. The decisions made in the heat of competition, the allure of shortcuts, and the relentless pursuit of the next big thing must all be tempered by a deeper understanding of the responsibilities that come with wielding such powerful tools.

## Redemption and Rebuilding

The days following Innovatech's launch were some of the darkest in Acme's history. The initial shock of seeing their own ideas paraded as someone else's victory left the company shaken at its core. Yet, as the shock wore off and the dust began to settle, a new purpose took root within Acme's walls. The crisis had exposed their vulnerabilities but also illuminated their resilience, their hunger for learning, and their unwavering belief in the power of innovation.

Thad, once consumed by guilt, now sat in his office typing with resolve. He was crafting a Correction of Error (COE) document, a confession of past mistakes and a roadmap for the future. This wasn't just about accountability; it was about making Acme stronger and smarter. Cleo Catchall entered Thad's office, a warm smile on her face. *"How's it coming along?"* she asked, glancing at the screen. Thad looked up, returning the smile. *"It's coming together. I want it to be honest. I want to share what went wrong and how we'll make it right."* Cleo nodded, taking a seat across from him. *"Yes, we've all learned some interesting lessons from all of this. Now, we just need to make sure we don't' make the same mistakes twice."*

Sparks strode in, a stack of papers in hand and a glimmer of optimism in his step. *"How are my two favorite problem-solvers doing?"*

Thad chuckled. "Finishing the COE doc." Sparks nodded. "Good. It's going to be key to our recovery, but it's just one piece of the puzzle."

Cleo leaned forward, her excitement bubbling. "We've got big plans. We're bringing in an AI consultant to craft a comprehensive policy and strategy. No more blind spots. We'll set guardrails, train the team, and understand the tools we're using—their strengths, their limits, and how to wield them responsibly." Thad added, "We're also launching Acme's first AI advisory board. Experts from every corner of the company will guide us, not just to avoid another crisis but to lead in responsible AI use."

Sparks beamed. "Exactly. This isn't just about fixing mistakes; it's about building something lasting. You two are leading the charge, and I couldn't be prouder."

The COE document didn't gather dust. It became the cornerstone of a company-wide transformation, sparking lunch-and-learns and honest discussions in every department. Acme brought in an AI consultant who helped map their readiness, identify gaps, and craft a policy built on ethics and foresight. The AI advisory board became a brain trust for responsible innovation, ensuring Acme would never stumble in the dark again.

Outside Acme, the world kept spinning, though not always gracefully. The injunction, though filed with high hopes, floundered in court. AI's shiny-newness and legal ambiguity left the ruling in Innovatech's favor. Meanwhile, Victoria Keen of WidgetWorks unraveled spectacularly in a storm of deceit and embezzlement, shuttering her company in scandal.

In contrast, Ptolemy Gauched of Titan Tech, LLC, proved the value of patience. He championed an "AI Readiness First" approach, crafting policies, training employees, and fortifying infrastructure with meticulous care. Titan Tech wasn't just cautious;

they were deliberate, a shining example of innovation done responsibly.

Back at Acme, the storm gave way to reinvention. The company's stumble became their first attempt in learning—not failure, but a foundation. And then came the moment of magic. Thad stood before a room buzzing with anticipation, unveiling Acme's groundbreaking new widget. The screen behind him glowed with its image, a marvel so ingenious it left the crowd spellbound. RABBIT AI, their trusted generative AI tool, had been wielded like a scalpel, not a sledgehammer, enhancing human creativity without overshadowing it. Sales exploded within hours of launch. Social media couldn't stop talking about it. Analysts called it revolutionary, and customers called it indispensable. Acme, once teetering on the edge of irrelevance, now stood proudly at the forefront of innovation.

As Thad looked out at the crowd, their eyes wide with wonder, his heart swelled. This widget wasn't just a widget—it was redemption, sculpted in metal and plastic. Proof that Acme could stumble and rise again. Proof that innovation and responsibility could waltz gracefully together. Proof that when lessons learned meet creativity unleashed, the result isn't just something new—it's something unforgettable.

## Chapter Summary

Acme Inc.'s team faces their worst fears as Innovatech reveals a sleek new widget at a highly publicized Silicon Valley launch—a product unmistakably based on Acme's proprietary designs, leaked through Thad's earlier misuse of AI tools. While their legal injunction fails to hold up in court due to the complexities of AI law, Acme refuses to back down. Rallying together, Cleo, Thad, and Sparks focus on controlling the narrative and preparing a counter-launch. Their perseverance pays off with the debut of their own groundbreaking widget, a marvel powered by the responsible use of Rabbit AI, which catapults Acme back to the forefront of innovation.

### Key Takeaways

- Transparency and accountability are crucial for rebuilding trust after a crisis.
- Effective leadership involves creating actionable steps to address mistakes and prevent future issues.
- Collaboration and shared learning are essential for organizational recovery and growth.

## Reflection Exercise

Do you know your company's AI readiness level? Take a simple AI readiness assessment and discover your company's score. Then write a reflection regarding your score. Access the assessment: bit.ly/aireadinesscore Or can the QR code:

### Critical Thinking Questions

1. What safeguards could have prevented the situation that Thad created?

2. Reflect on Thad's transformation. How did taking accountability for his actions help him grow as a professional?

-

-

-

3. What leadership qualities did Cleo, Thad, and Sparks demonstrate, and how did it influence Acme's long-term recovery?

-

## Practical Applications

**Create a Crisis Response Playbook**: Draft a playbook for your organization, including steps for addressing a major crisis and rebuilding trust

**Host a "Lessons Learned" Session**: Organize a meeting (real or hypothetical) to share mistakes and outline strategies for preventing similar issues.

**Develop an Accountability Framework**: Write down steps your team or organization can take to ensure mistakes are acknowledged and turned into learning opportunities. Here's an example:

- **Mistake Identified** → Employee or team reports the issue.
- **Mistake Reviewed** → Conduct a review - we listen and we don't judge.
- **Lessons Learned Documented** → The root cause and corrective actions that were taken are recorded (i.e. *correction of error*)
- Company Updates Completed and Shared

  Policies and training are updated.
- **Feedback Gathered** → Follow-up surveys or reviews ensure the actions taken were effective.

## Your Notes

## DR. A'S Closing Remarks

Ah, dear reader, it is I, Dr. Arym Basilia Radlon-Manjai de Fernandez, Dr. A, you trusted, always insightful guide through the twists and turns of this little tale. And what a tale it has been! We've laughed, we've cried, we've gasped in shock as secrets were spilled and fortunes teetered on the edge of oblivion. But, as the final curtain falls, it's time to take a step back, powder our noses, and reflect on the wild ride we've just been on.

Let's recap, shall we? We began our story with Thaddeus Blandly, a man so delightfully average that his name could be a synonym for *invisible,* who stumbled upon the shiny new toy that is CHATTERBOTGPT. In his eagerness to make his mark, Thad dove headfirst into the world of generative AI without so much as a second thought about the consequences. And oh, what consequences there were! Before he knew it, Acme Inc.'s crown jewels-- its top-secret designs-- were scattered to the winds, leaving our dear company teetering on the brink of disaster.

But fear not, for where there is chaos, there is opportunity! Enter Cleo Catchall, the unflappable heroine who kept her wits about her even as the storm clouds gathered. With her sharp mind and even sharper instincts, Cleo navigated the murky waters of crisis management, helping Acme not just survive, but thrive. And let's not forget Edison Sparks, whose boundless enthusiasm for all things new and shiny was tempered by a newfound appreciation for caution and strategy.

Together, this trio turned their darkest hour into a springboard for innovation and growth. They brought in an AI consultant, established Acme's first

AI advisory board, and-- perhaps most importantly-- shared their hard-won lessons with the entire company, ensuring that the mistakes of the past would not be repeated.

But, my dear reader, this isn't just a story about Acme Inc. and its merry band of misfits. No, no, no; this is a story with a message, a cautionary tale for anyone who finds themselves tempted by the glittering promises of generative AI without fully understanding the shadows that lurk beneath.

Now, let's be honest; who among us hasn't felt the siren call of convenience? The allure of a free tool that promises to do all the heavy lifting for you, leaving you to bask in the glow of effortless brilliance. But, darling, let me be clear: there is no such thing as a free lunch, especially when it comes to your company's most valuable assets.

So, before you go clicking <upload> and handing over your data to some mysterious digital entity, consider this: do you really know how that data will be used? Have you read the fine print? Do you understand where your information is going, how it's being stored, and who might have access to it? If the answer to any of these questions is No, then I implore you to step away from the keyboard and take a deep breath.

Here are a few strategies to keep you on the right path:

**1. Read the Terms and Conditions**: Yes, darling, I know it's tedious, but those pesky terms and conditions are there for a reason. Understand what you're agreeing to before you hand over your data.

**2. Consult with Experts:** If you're not sure about a tool, don't be afraid to ask someone who is. Bring in a consultant, talk to your IT department, or gather your AI advisory board. Knowledge is power, and in this case, it might just save your company.

**3. Use Secure, Trusted Platforms:** Free tools are tempting, but they're not always the safest option. Invest in secure, trusted platforms that offer transparency about how your data is managed and stored.

**4. Develop an AI Policy:** Don't wait for a crisis to strike; be proactive! Establish clear guidelines for how AI tools can be used within your company, and make sure everyone understands the risks involved.

**5. Educate Your Team:** Make sure everyone in your company understands the potential risks of using generative AI tools. Host lunch-and-learns, create resources, and foster a culture of awareness.

And now, for the moral of our story, the lesson that lies at the heart of all the drama, the triumphs, and the missteps: Innovation is a marvelous, thrilling endeavor, but it is not without its perils. The tools we use are only as effective as the care we take in wielding them. So, be bold, be daring, but also be wise. For in the world of technology, the line between brilliance and disaster is often as thin as a digital thread.

As our story comes to an end, I leave you with this: the journey of innovation is never truly over. It is a continuous dance, a delicate balancing act between risk and reward, between caution and creativity. And whether you're leading a company or simply navigating the ever-changing landscape of technology, remember that the greatest innovations come not from shortcuts, but from a deep understanding of the tools we use and the responsibility that comes with them.

Until we meet again, I remain your ever-watchful, always dramatic narrator, Dr. A. Now, go forth and innovate, but do so wisely, my dear reader, do so wisely.

# Epilogue

As the CEO and founder of UnDesto AI, I've had the privilege—and sometimes the frustration—of witnessing firsthand the messy, complicated ways businesses approach artificial intelligence. Many of the events in this book, while fictionalized and exaggerated for storytelling purposes, are inspired by real-life scenarios I've encountered or had shared with me in my role as an Applied AI Engineer and Consultant.

I've heard executives proudly describe how they used a personal ChatGPT license to upload sensitive company data to forecast strategies or draft reports, completely unaware of the potential risks to their intellectual property and data security. I've also listened to countless employees explain how they circumvented their organization's AI restrictions by emailing work to their personal accounts, using generative AI tools on their own devices, and sending the results back to their work email. These stories may seem outlandish, but they are far more common than you might think.

According recent data, 72% of companies do not have an AI policy or strategy in place[1]. Which means that employees have no guardrails for the use and implementation of AI within their workflow

It's because of scenarios like these that UnDesto AI exists. At UnDesto, we focus on helping businesses

---

[1] Houter, B. K. D. (2024, November 12). AI in the Workplace: Answering 3 Big Questions. Gallup.com. bit.ly/4hokwFO.

understand their AI readiness level across four critical domains:

1. **Leadership and AI Strategy**: Ensuring leaders are equipped with the knowledge to make informed decisions about AI adoption and integration.
2. **Change Management and Operations**: Guiding teams through the cultural and operational shifts required to implement AI effectively.
3. **Product and Service Innovation**: Leveraging AI to enhance offerings while staying aligned with ethical and practical standards.
4. **Customer-Focused AI Solutions**: Designing AI initiatives that prioritize customer trust, security, and value.

At UnDesto AI, we prioritize AI readiness, comprehensive staff training, and the implementation of Frugal AI strategies. Our approach encourages organizations to maximize the potential of their existing tools and systems before investing heavily in new solutions. We believe in smart, sustainable AI adoption that aligns with our clients' current infrastructure and business goals.

Our mission is to help companies transform AI challenges into opportunities for growth and innovation.

So, I hope this book serves as a conversation starter and a practical guide for businesses, educators, and students alike. Whether you're just beginning to explore AI or are grappling with its complexities, my goal is to provide you with insights, inspiration, and a little humor along the way.

Thank you for allowing me to share this journey with you. Here's to building a future where innovation and responsibility go hand in hand.

Warm regards,

Myra Roldan

Founder & CEO, UnDesto AI

# Resources

## Glossary of Key Terms

**Artificial Intelligence (AI)**: The theory and development of computer systems able to perform tasks that normally require human intelligence, such as visual perception,

speech recognition, decision-making, and translation between languages.

**ChatterBotGPT**: A fictional AI tool in the story, used to generate creative content from user text prompts, similar to generative AI tools available today.

**Generative AI**: A type of artificial intelligence that can generate various kinds of data, such as text, images, audio, and video, based on user prompts or input data.

**Sillycon Valley**: A fictionalized version of Silicon Valley, used in the story to satirize the tech industry and its culture.

**Terms of Service**: A legal document outlining the rules and conditions for using a particular service, application, or product, especially for software.

**Data Breach:** A security incident in which sensitive, protected, or confidential data is copied, transmitted, viewed, stolen, or used by an unauthorized individual or entity.

**Injunction:** A court order that requires a party to do or refrain from doing specific acts that could cause damage to another person.

**Declaratory Judgment**: A court ruling that clarifies the legal rights and responsibilities of parties involved in a dispute, without requiring them to take any specific action.

**Trade Secrets:** Confidential information that businesses use to gain a competitive advantage and are protected by law against unauthorized use or disclosure.

**Correction of Error (COE)**: A document that details errors and oversights, and what was learned from the error.

**Prompt Engineering**: The process of crafting effective instructions or queries for an AI model to elicit desired outputs, which in the story is described as *magic notes.*

## Book Club Discussion Questions

1. What is the central conflict of the story, and how does it relate to the use of AI?
2. How does the book critique the tech industry and its approach to innovation?
3. What are the main consequences of Thad's actions and how do they impact Acme Inc.?
4. What are some key lessons or takeaways regarding the use of AI that are highlighted in this book?
5. How does the story explore the theme of "redemption" in the aftermath of the crisis?
6. How does the narrative style contribute to the book's overall message?
7. Discuss the role of both optimism and naiveté in the story, focusing on how Thad

## Student Essay Questions

1. Blandly's personality traits lead to both innovative breakthroughs and significant setbacks.
2. Analyze the author's use of the character Dr. A as a narrator. How does her unique perspective and commentary enhance the reader's understanding of the themes of innovation and technology?
3. Explore the concept of "shortcuts" in the context of the story, and explain how the pursuit of quick results can lead to unintended consequences. Consider other instances in which shortcuts have created trouble in history and other narratives.
4. Examine the role of competition in the tech industry as portrayed in this story. How does the drive to stay ahead of rivals both inspire and corrupt innovative processes?
5. In what ways does the story use the narrative device of fortune cookies to foreshadow events, comment on Thad's state of mind, or raise questions about fate versus free will?

# Acknowledgments

This book is the result of collaboration, creativity, and dedication from many individuals and tools, each contributing their unique skills and expertise. I extend my heartfelt gratitude to:

- **OpenAI ChatGPT** for providing insightful edits and helping shape the tone of the initial drafts of this book with precision and clarity.
- **Nicole Papaioannou,** who meticulously proofed and edited the manuscript, ensuring its readability and polish.
- **Ideogram AI,** for creating the beautiful and thoughtful interior illustrations that bring the concepts to life.
- **Muhammad Arslan,** for designing the striking book cover that captures the essence of this work. You can find more of Muhammad's incredible work on Fiverr: arshgfx.

To everyone who supported me throughout this journey, thank you for your encouragement and belief in this project. This book would not have been possible without you

# About the Author

Myra is the founder and CEO of UnDesto AI™, a boutique consulting firm dedicated to helping companies harness the power of artificial intelligence. Through UnDesto, she has developed innovative tools that assess AI readiness and guide organizations in building the infrastructure, strategies, and data frameworks needed to successfully integrate AI solutions aligned with their business goals. As the co-founder of YourAcademy.ai, Myra also works to transform education, equipping learners and educators with the skills and tools for the future of work. A TEDx speaker, author, and international presenter, Myra is known for making cutting-edge technologies accessible and impactful, combining over 20 years of tech expertise with her gift for simplifying complex ideas.

Beyond her work in consulting and education, Myra is a tireless advocate for inclusive innovation and a proud mom to three talented daughters. Whether she's inspiring audiences to embrace AI, guiding organizations toward smarter decisions, or championing diverse voices in tech, Myra leads with intention, empathy, and a commitment to unlocking human potential.

**UnDesto AI®**

UnDesto AI® equips organizations with the strategy, tools, and talent they need to confidently lead in the age of artificial intelligence. We help businesses move beyond experimentation to meaningful execution by offering end-to-end AI consulting and services tailored to your goals.

**Our services include:**

- **AI Strategy and Executive Advisory:** Guiding leadership teams in building actionable roadmaps aligned with business priorities.
- **AI Policy Development:** Creating responsible, future-ready policies that protect data, people, and reputation.
- **Training and Enablement:** Equipping teams with the skills and mindset needed to integrate AI into daily work.
- **AI Automation and Agent Development:** Designing and deploying AI solutions that streamline workflows and accelerate productivity.
- **Data Management:** Ensuring your data is clean, structured, and ready for responsible AI use.

- **Fractional Chief AI Officer Services:** Providing strategic leadership without the overhead of a full-time hire.
- **Fractional Operations Support:** Delivering operational expertise to implement AI initiatives efficiently across departments and teams.

Whether you're just beginning your AI journey or ready to scale, UnDesto AI® offers the clarity, experience, and hands-on support you need to move forward with confidence.

Contact Us:

**https://undesto.ai**

**hello@undesto.ai**

www.ingramcontent.com/pod-product-compliance
Lightning Source LLC
LaVergne TN
LVHW022052200926
848481LV00003B/885